About the Author

Irene Daria, Ph.D. is a developmental psychologist who specializes in teaching children how to read.

In addition to teaching the children of many celebrities to read, she has taught hundreds of other children—both as a paid specialist and as a volunteer—and has trained teachers in the science of reading.

A passionate literacy advocate, Dr. Daria is the founder and director of Steps Tutoring in New York City. Her *Steps to Reading* workbook series will enable you to teach a child how to read using the same research-based, fun, and effective methods Dr. Daria uses in her renown private lessons.

For more information, visit:
www.StepsTutoring.com or www.StepstoReading.com

Bulk discounts are available. Please email: info@StepsPublishing.com

For more information about Steps to Reading see:

www.StepstoReading.com

Copyright © 2024 by STEPS Publishing, Inc. All rights reserved. No part of this book may be reproduced or utilized in any form or by any electronic or mechanical means, including photocopying, without permission in writing from the publisher.

Printed in the U.S.A.
ISBN 978-0-9864329-9-6

Book 4

STEPS to...
Reading

by Irene Daria, Ph.D.

Illustrations by Tingting Wei, Eryka Sajek and Eric Wiener

Table of Contents

Long a .... Pg. 2

Long i .... Pg. 33

Long o .... Pg. 57

Long u .... Pg. 79

Vowels at the end of little words .... Pg. 100

Y at the end of little words .... Pg. 108

Y at the end of longer words .... Pg. 118

What this book teaches

This is Book 4 in the *Steps to Reading* series. It teaches long vowels, as well as the sounds vowels and y make when they are at the end of a word. Long vowels are the sounds vowels make in words like "cane," "pine," and "cone." In these words, the first vowel "says its name," or "makes its alphabet sound," and the e at the end is silent.

Book 4 builds on the phonics skills taught in the first three *Steps to Reading* books. Book 1 in the series teaches short vowel sounds; Book 2 teaches blends; and Book 3 teaches digraphs. Digraphs are the sounds made by the letters --ch, --sh, -th, and --wh. If your student has not yet mastered these phonics rules, it would be best to complete the earlier books in the series before moving on to this book.

Supplemental materials

The books listed below are great practice for the skills your student will be learning as he or she progresses through the lessons in this book. I highly recommend getting them when you begin this book because your student will be reading them very soon!

"Primary Phonics," Set 2A by Barbara Makar. This is a set of 10 stories published by Educators Publishing Service.

"Now I'm Reading! Level 2: Snack Attack," by Nora Gaydos. This is an adorable set of early readers available as an e-book from Random House.

"Dishy-Washy," by Joy Cowley. Published by Mc-Graw Hill Education.

"Dick and Jane: Go, Go, Go." Published by Penguin Young Readers.

"Dick and Jane: Go Away, Spot." Published by Penguin Young Readers.

Step 1   Silent e

| Instructions |

This book teaches the long vowel sounds. These are the sounds vowels make in words like "cane," "pine," and "cone." Children find the idea of "long" and "short vowels" very confusing. For that reason, you will not be using those phrases with your student. Instead, you will introduce your student to long vowels by doing the following...

1. Start by pointing at the child and asking, **"What's your name?"**
2. Give the child a chance to answer.
3. Then point to yourself and say, **"What's my name?"**
4. Give the child a chance to answer.
5. Now, point to the letter "a" (*on the opposite page*) and say, **"What is that letter's name?"**
6. The child should say, "A," just as he or she would when identifying the letter in the alphabet.
7. Say, **"Right. Just like we have names, letters have names. Their names are the sounds you say when you recite the alphabet."**
8. Again, point to the letter "a" (*on the opposite page*) and say, **"This letter's name is `a.' You're going on to a whole new step in reading now. You're going to learn words in which the letter 'a' says its name. A vowel will say its name when there is a silent e at the end of a word. It's called silent e because it doesn't make a sound. It's only placed at the end of a word so that it can exert its power and make the other vowel say its name. Silent e is such a powerful letter that some people call it magic e. Let's take a look at this movie."**
9. Play the silent e movie on www.starfall.com. Click on "Kindergarten," then "Learn to Read." This is the second item in the main menu. Then scroll down the "Movies" section on the right hand side of the screen until you see the link for the silent e movie.

This letter's name is 'a'

Instructions

Say: "**This letter's name is 'a.'** When a vowel says its name, it makes the same sound it makes when you recite the alphabet."

Silent e works its magic

Instructions

1. Point to the word "can," *right*.
2. Say, **"What is that word?"**
3. The child should say "can."

Instructions

1. Say, **"Very good. Now look what happens when we add 'e' to the end of can."**
2. Write the letter "e" on the line, *right*.
3. Say, **"Silent e turned 'can' into a totally different word without even making a sound."**

Instructions

1. Say, **"Silent e turned the word 'can' into 'cane.' Isn't that cool?"**

Instructions

1. Point to the word "cane" in the box, *right*.
2. Say, **"Now you read it."**
3. The child should read the word "cane."

Silent e makes "a" say its name

"a" says its name in "gate"

Instructions

Say to the child: "**Silent e makes 'a' say its name in words like 'gate,' 'game,' and 'tape.'**"

Write and read the word

Read	Write silent e on the line	Silent e makes a say its name	Read
can	can_e_	cane	cane
cap	cap __	cape	cape
mad	mad __	made	made
Jan	Jan __	Jane	Jane
tap	tap __	tape	tape

Which word is it?

Say: "Read each word out loud. Circle the word that goes with the picture."

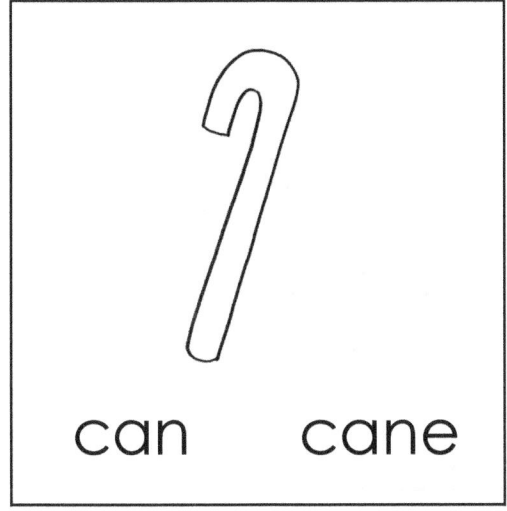
can   cane

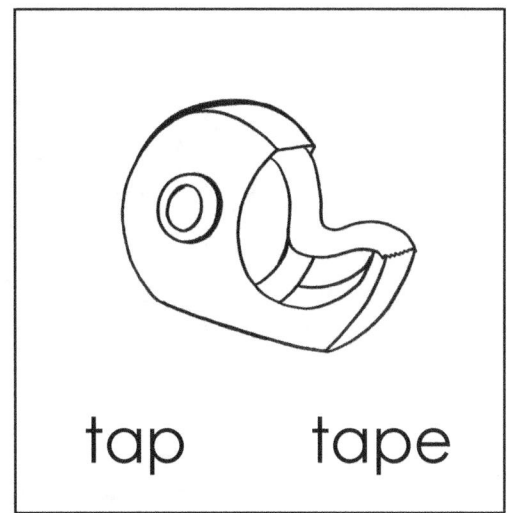
tap   tape

mad   made

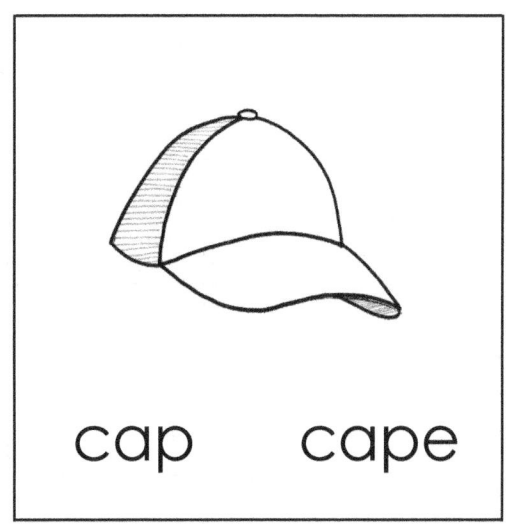
cap   cape

Write words in which "a" says its name

Say: **"Write 'a' on the blank lines and read the words out loud."**

t_ke	b_ke
m_ke	n_me
s_ve	c_ke
f_ke	g_te

Draw a line from the word to the picture

Say: "**Read each word out loud. Then draw a line from the correct word to the picture.**"

save tap tape 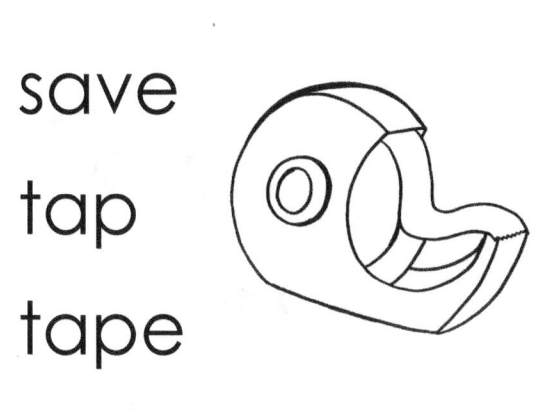	made gate make
cave bake fake 	cake take date 
safe brave game 	lake shave late 

9

Write the word and circle the picture

Say: "**Read the word out loud.** Then write the word, and circle the picture that shows the word."

tape

___ ___ ___ ___

game

___ ___ ___ ___

cake

___ ___ ___ ___

gate

___ ___ ___ ___

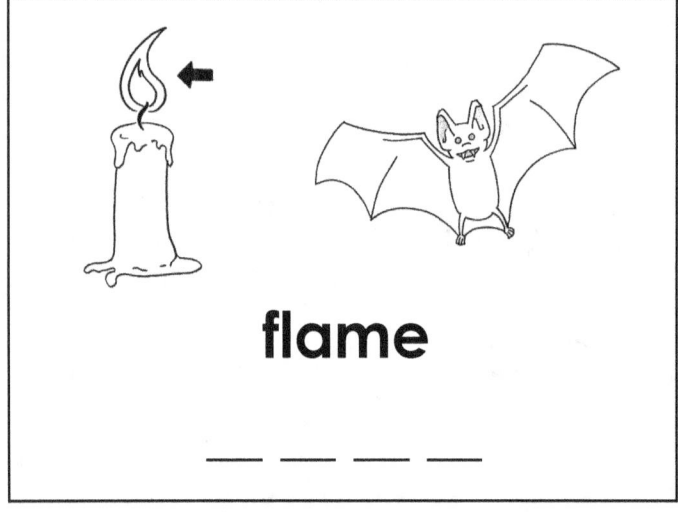

flame

___ ___ ___ ___ ___

grape

___ ___ ___ ___ ___

Which word is it?

Say: "**Read each word out loud. Circle the word that goes with the picture.**"

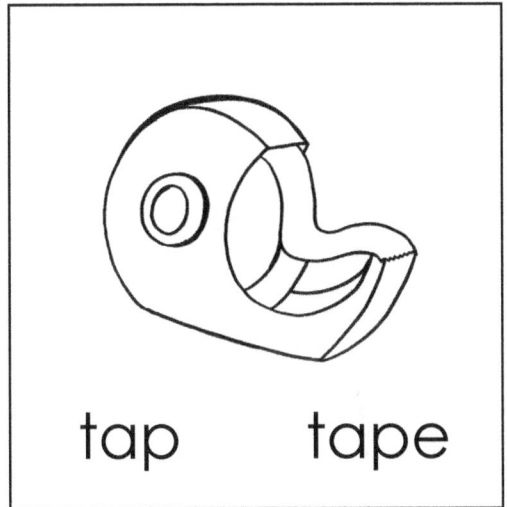

tap   tape

gate   got

game   came

lock   cake

lake   lock

back   bake

11

Play Bingo!

Instructions

Materials:
- Flashcards. Cut out the cards on the opposite page.
- 2 gameboards follow the flashcards. In Bingo, every player gets his or her own gameboard. You and the child should each select a gameboard to use.
- Pennies to use as game pieces.

1. Place the flashcards in one stack, with the words facing up.
2. Have the child read the word on the top card in the stack.
3. Each of you should look for that word on your Bingo boards and place a penny on top of the word on your boards when you find it.
4. Place the card the child read face down on the table.
5. Repeat steps 2-4. The child should be the one doing all of the reading of the words on the flashcards. Continue until one of you has five pennies in a row, either horizontally, vertically, or diagonally. The first player to get five in a row should call out, "Bingo!" That player wins the game.

Play Bingo!

cane	cape	made	tape

gate	make	game	bake	cake
rake	lake	vase	wave	save
late	cave	came	date	shave
safe	grape	brave	flame	crate

This page is intentionally blank.

This page is intentionally blank.

BINGO

cane	make	lake	tape	game
vase	save	cape	came	wave
late	grape	✗	made	date
gate	crate	bake	safe	cake
shave	flame	rake	cave	brave

BINGO

cane	cape	made	tape	gate
make	game	bake	cake	rake
lake	vase	✗	wave	save
late	cave	came	date	shave
safe	grape	brave	flame	crate

Step 2

What you need to know about...
Sight Words

Sight Words are words the child needs to memorize, as opposed to sound out. Sight words either do not follow phonics rules (and, therefore, cannot be sounded out) or they are very common words that follow phonics rules the child has not yet learned.

The sight words in this book are presented in the order they will appear in the stories children will be reading as they make their way through this book. I call them Power Words because knowing how to read these sight words will increase the child's reading power. Since these words are so common in stories, memorizing them will enable your child to read many books much more quickly.

If your student completed the first three books in the *Steps to Reading* series, then he or she knows the 28 most common sight words. (They are listed on the following pages.) If your student did not complete Books 1, 2, and 3, make sure your student knows those words.

First set of Power Words

the	has	off
is	to	his
on	was	dog
as	of	for

Second set of Power Words

see	down	little
says	put	with
go	pull	look
no	full	said

Third set of Power Words

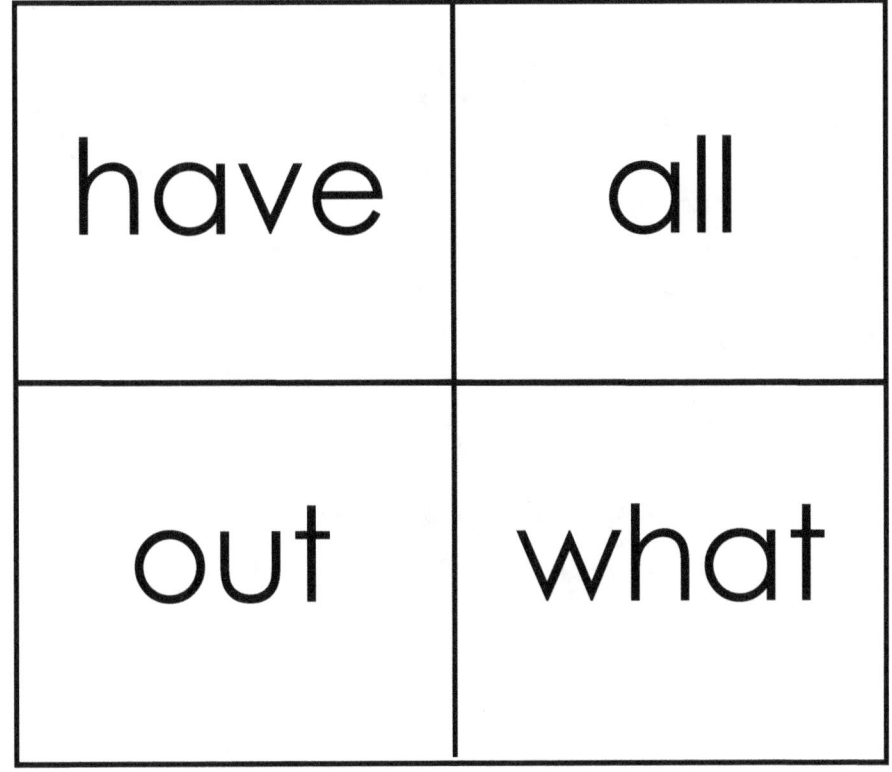

have	all
out	what

Power Word

Instructions

1. Say: "**Some words don't follow any of the sounding-out rules. They are words that just need to be memorized. We will call them Power Words because they are words that appear very often in the stories you will be reading. Knowing these words will really boost your reading power.**"
2. Point to the word "do," *above*. Say, "**This word is 'do.'**"
3. On the following page, your student will trace and write the word "do."
4. Any time you come to a Power Word lesson in this book, read the word to the child and have him or her trace and write the word on the lines that follow.

Write the Word

do

do

do

do

do

do

Play games on the computer!

Instructions

1. Go to www.starfall.com. Make sure your computer's sound is turned on.
2. Click on "Kindergarten" and then "Learn to Read."
3. In "Learn to Read, the left column is labeled, "Game." Go to row #6 and click on "Long A."
4. Have your student complete this picture hunt. Most kids really love playing this game.
5. After your student is done with the picture hunt, go back to row #6 and click on the game labeled, "Cane."

Solve the puzzle

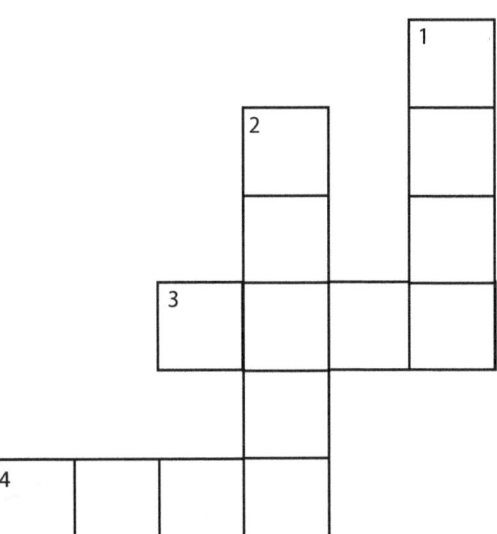

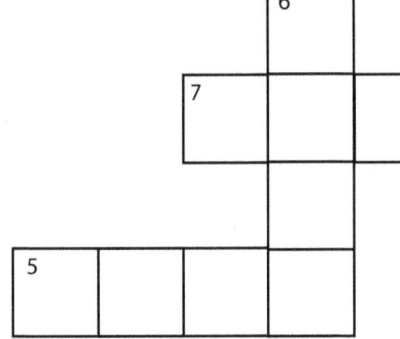

Word Box

late
gate
cane
cake
brave
game
make
tape

Across

3. Something you play.
4. Something you serve at a birthday party.
7. Another word for fence.

Down

1. To create something.
2. The opposite of scared.
4. A stick that helps older people walk.
5. You use it to attach something, usually paper.
6. Not on time.

Answers are on the following page.

25

Puzzle answers

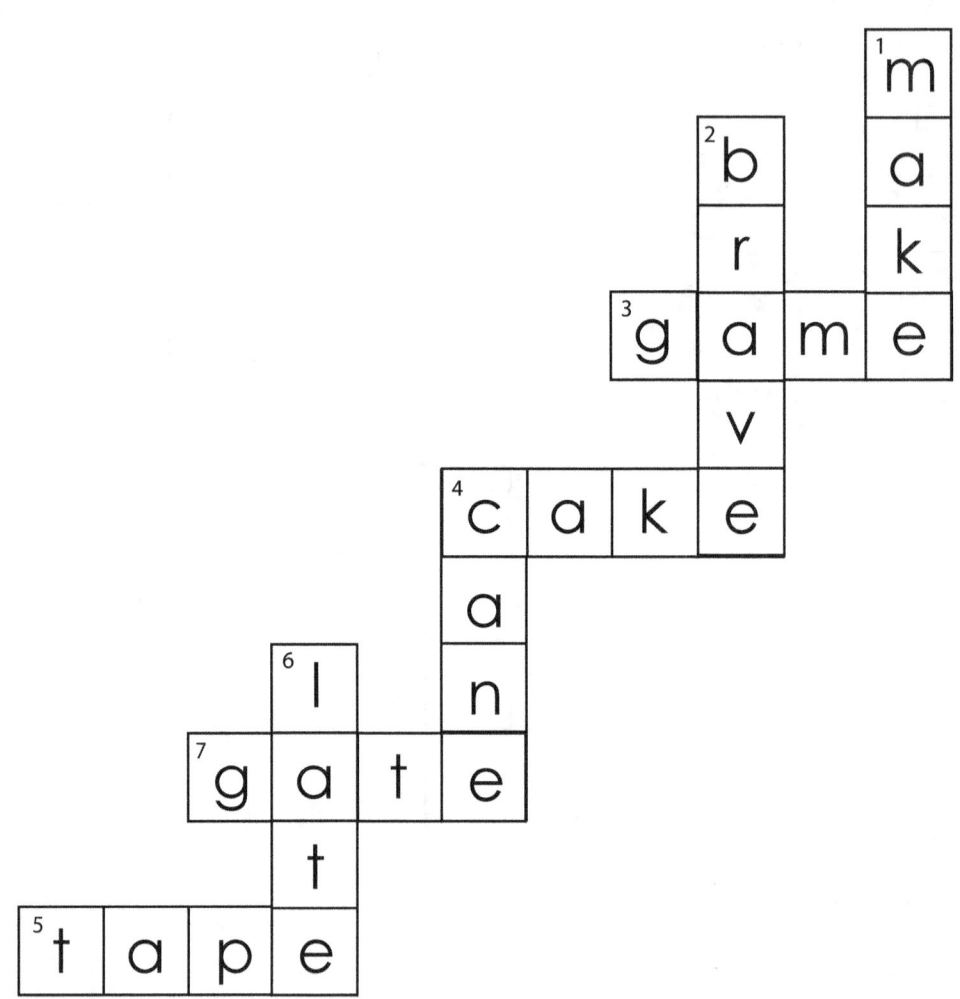

Circle the letters

Say: "**Circle the correct letters. Then write the word.**"
Tell the child the pictures show: bake, cake, wave, gate, tape, and vase.

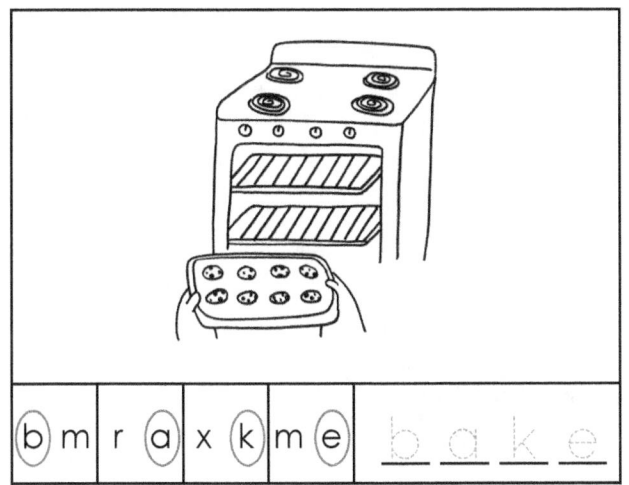

| ⓑ | m | r | ⓐ | x | ⓚ | m | ⓔ | b a k e |

| f | c | a | i | n | k | h | e | _ _ _ _ |

| w | s | h | a | x | v | m | e | _ _ _ _ |

| g | c | h | a | t | s | m | e | _ _ _ _ |

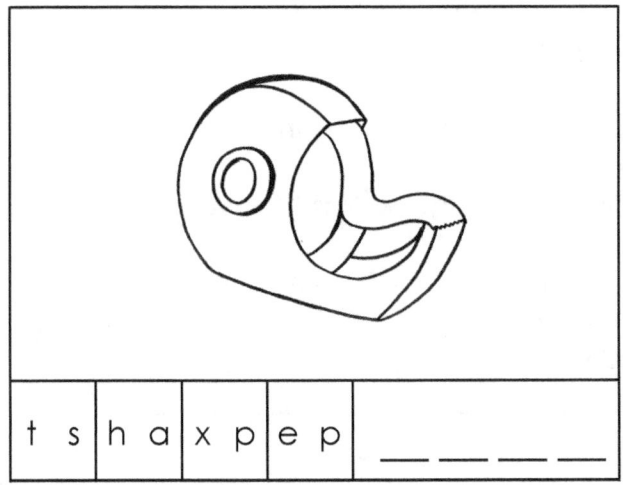

| t | s | h | a | x | p | e | p | _ _ _ _ |

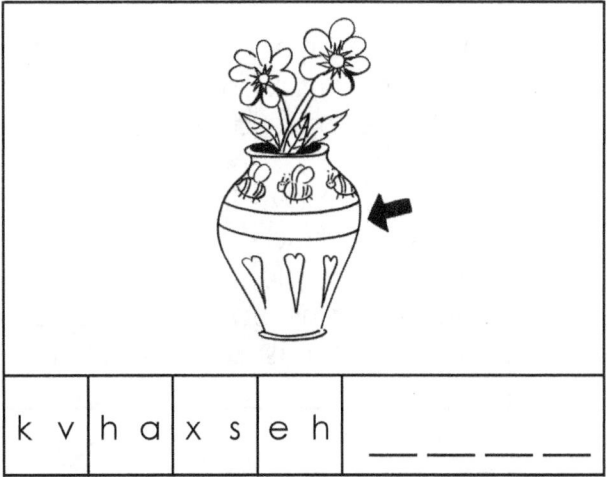

| k | v | h | a | x | s | e | h | _ _ _ _ |

Play a board game!

First one to reach the end wins!

Instructions

Materials you will need: • A single die.
 • Coins to use as markers.
 • Gameboard, *opposite page.*

1. Each player places a coin on "start."
2. Take turns rolling the die.
3. Move forward the same amount of spaces as the number on the die.
4. As you move forward on the board, read the words that you pass and land on.
5. For example, if a five comes up on the die, move five spaces on the game board and read five words.
6. The first person to reach the end wins.

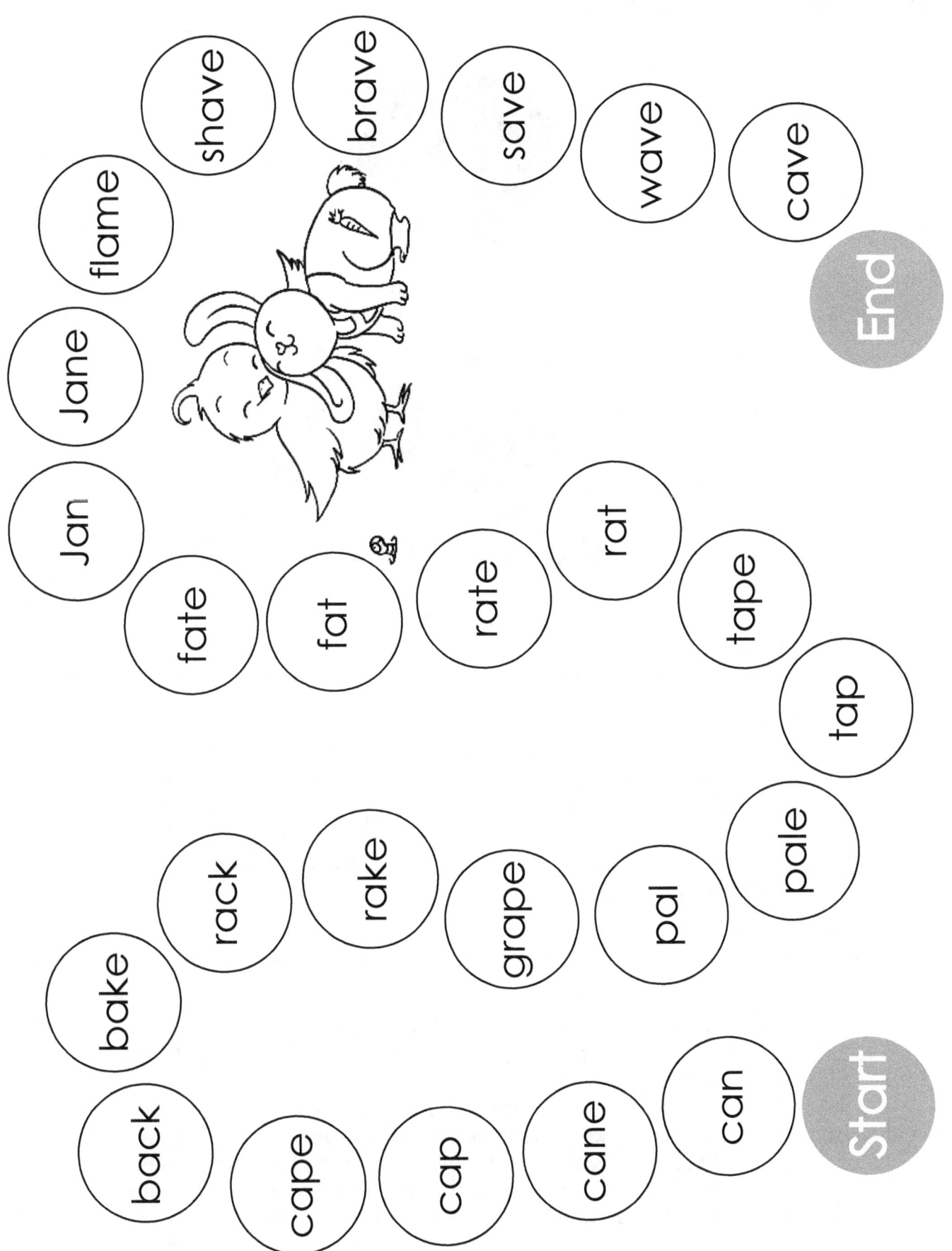

Read some stories!

Instructions

Read a book

- "Make the Bed," by Barbara W. Makar. This is Book 2 in Primary Phonics Set 2A. See page 1 ("Supplemental Materials") for more information.

- "Ape Shake." This is Book 6 in "Now I'm Reading, Level 2: Snack Attack," by Nora Gaydos.

Read online

1. Go to www.starfall.com.
2. Click on "Kindergarten" and then on "Learn to Read."
3. Click on Story 6, "Jake's Tale," in the column that says, "Book." Make sure the computer's sound is on.
4. Tell the child to read the sentence that appears on the screen for each page. Don't let him click on the individual words because, if he does, the computer will read the words for him. You want the child to do all the reading. After he is done reading each sentence, he can click on the picture above it. The picture will then move in a delightful way.

Find the words

The words listed in the box are hidden in the puzzle below. Look for them going down, up, or diagonally. Circle the words when you find them.

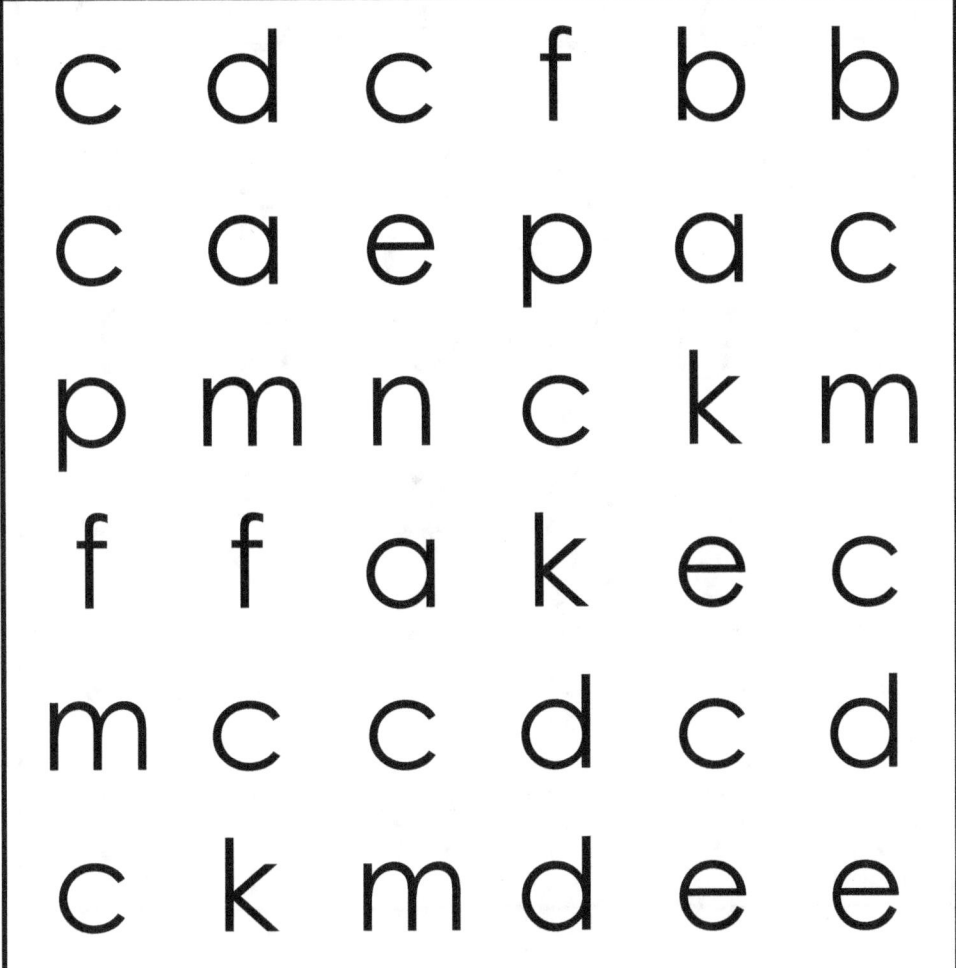

Word box
can
cane
cap
cape
mad
made
bake
fake

Answers

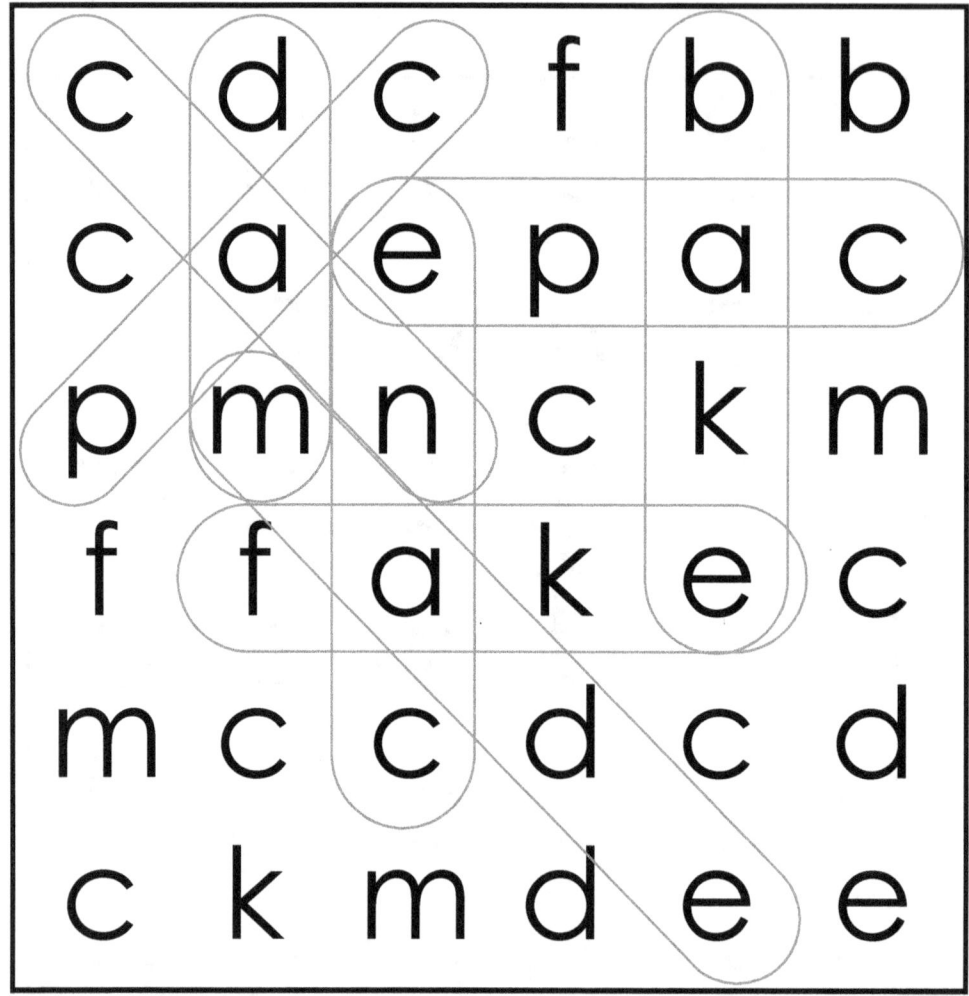

Step 3   Silent e makes "i" say its name

'i' says its name in "bike"

Instructions

Say to the child: "**Silent e makes 'i' say its name in words like 'like,' 'bike,' and 'hide.'**"

Write and read the word

Read	Write silent e on the line	Silent e makes a say its name	Read
bit	bit_e_	bite	bite
kit	kit __	kite	kite
hid	hid __	hide	hide
rid	rid __	ride	ride
dim	dim __	dime	dime
fin	fin __	fine	fine
pin	pin __	pine	pine

Which word is it?

Say: **"Read each word out loud. Circle the word that goes with the picture."**

pin   pine

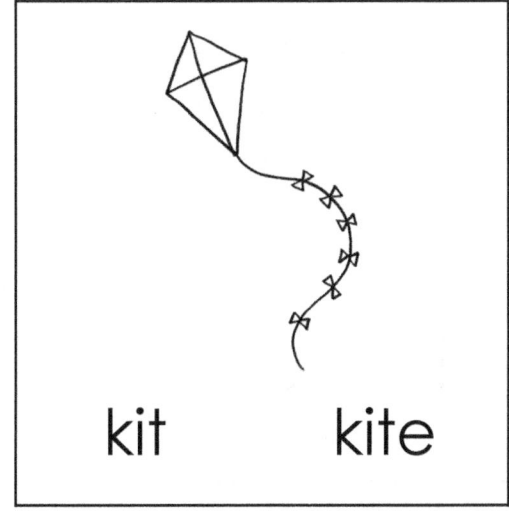
kit   kite

fin   fine

dim   dime

Tim   time

35

Write words in which "i" says its name

Say: **"Write 'i' on the blank lines and read the words out loud."**

b_te	h_de
f_ne	b_ke
d_ve	l_ne
w_re	v_ne

Draw a line from the word to the picture

Say: "**Read each word out loud. Then draw a line from the correct word to the picture.**"

five fit flame 	Dave dive drive 
hill hive help 	kit kite came 
nine gave drive 	dim dime game 

Write the word and circle the picture

Say: "Read the word out loud. Then write the word, and circle the picture that shows the word."

bike

_ _ _ _

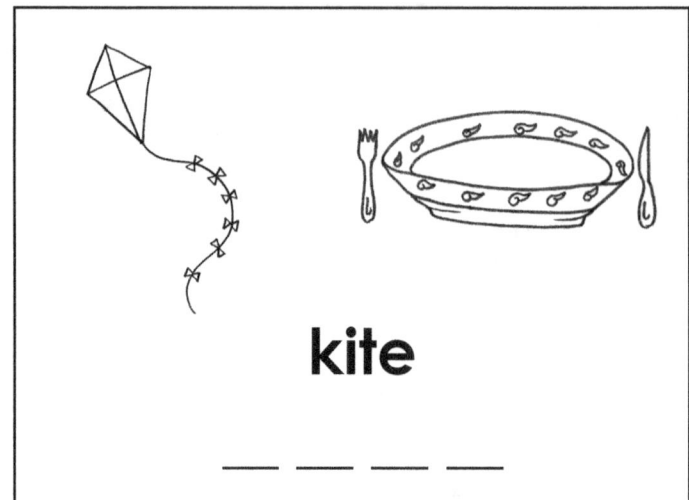

kite

_ _ _ _

hive

_ _ _ _

dime

_ _ _ _

five

_ _ _ _

dive

_ _ _ _

Which word is it?

Say: "**Read each word out loud. Circle the word that goes with the picture.**"

line   bike

hive   hill

kick   kite

hive   dive

nine   name

vine   pine

39

Play Bingo!

Instructions

Materials: • Flashcards. Cut out the cards on the opposite page.
• 2 gameboards follow the flashcards. In Bingo, every player gets his or her own gameboard. You and the child should each select a gameboard to use.
• Pennies to use as game pieces.

1. Place the flashcards in one stack, with the words facing up.
2. Have the child read the word on the top card in the stack.
3. Each of you should look for that word on your Bingo boards and place a penny on top of the word on your boards when you find it.
4. Place the card the child read face down on the table.
5. Repeat steps 2-4. The child should be the one doing all of the reading of the words on the flashcards. Continue until one of you has five pennies in a row, either horizontally, vertically, or diagonally. The first player to get five in a row should call out, "Bingo!" That player wins the game.

Play Bingo!

bake	bike	cane	bit	
cape	bite	made	kit	Jane
kite	hide	fine	vine	brave
shade	bride	drive	Kate	time
lime	line	came	game	shave

This page is intentionally blank.

This page is intentionally blank.

BINGO

bake	bike	cane	bit	cape
bite	made	kit	Jane	kite
hide	fine	✕	vine	brave
shade	bride	drive	Kate	time
lime	line	came	game	shave

BINGO

cane	bite	brave	kite	shade
fine	bake	came	bride	game
Jane	vine	✕	bit	shave
bike	Kate	line	hide	lime
fine	kit	cape	drive	made

Step 4 Power Word

you

you

you

you

Does the sentence make sense?

Say: "**Read each sentence out loud. Color in the smiley face if the sentence makes sense, and the frown if it does not.**"

| Do you like to bake a cake for fun? | ☺ ☹ |

| Do you think a cat can fix a box with tape? | ☺ ☹ |

| Do you like to bake fish? | ☺ ☹ |

| Do you wish to drive your bike on the line? | ☺ ☹ |

| Do you like to save a fake grape? | ☺ ☹ |

| Do you want to take a bike on the lake? | ☺ ☹ |

| Do you like a snake at the gate? | ☺ ☹ |

| Do you wish for a dog as a pet? | ☺ ☹ |

Play a board game!

First one to reach the end wins!

Instructions

<u>Materials you will need</u>: • A single die.
• Coins to use as markers.
• Gameboard, *opposite page*.

1. Each player places a coin on "start."
2. Take turns rolling the die.
3. Move forward the same amount of spaces as the number on the die.
4. As you move forward on the board, read the words that you pass and land on.
5. For example, if a five comes up on the die, move five spaces on the game board and read five words.
6. The first person to reach the end wins.

Circle the letters

Say: "**Circle the correct letters. Then write the word.**"
Tell the child the pictures show: kite, hive, five, bike, dive, nine.

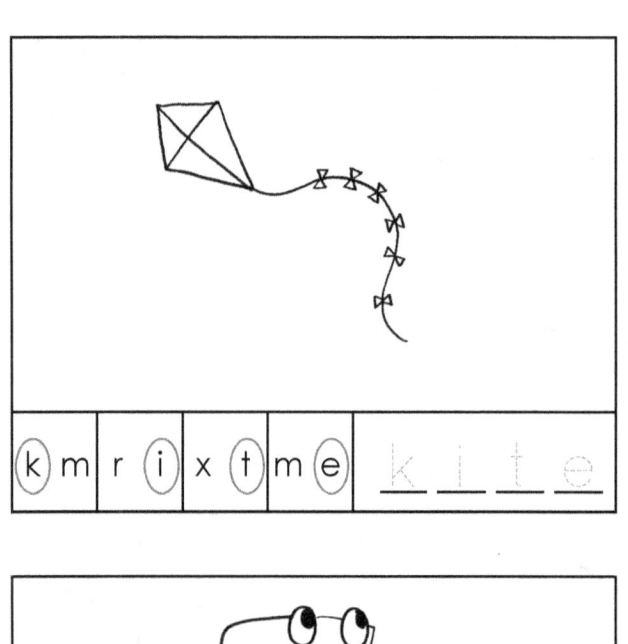

(k) m (r) (i) x (t) m (e)   k i t e

f h a i v k h e   _ _ _ _

f s h i x v m e   _ _ _ _

b c i a t k m e   _ _ _ _

d s h i v p e p   _ _ _ _

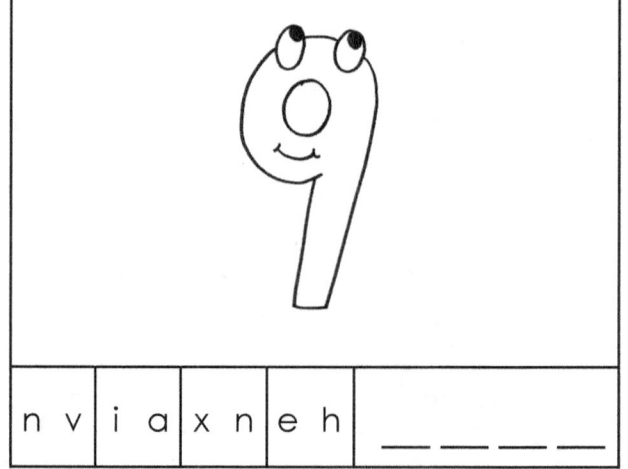

n v i a x n e h   _ _ _ _

Solve the puzzle

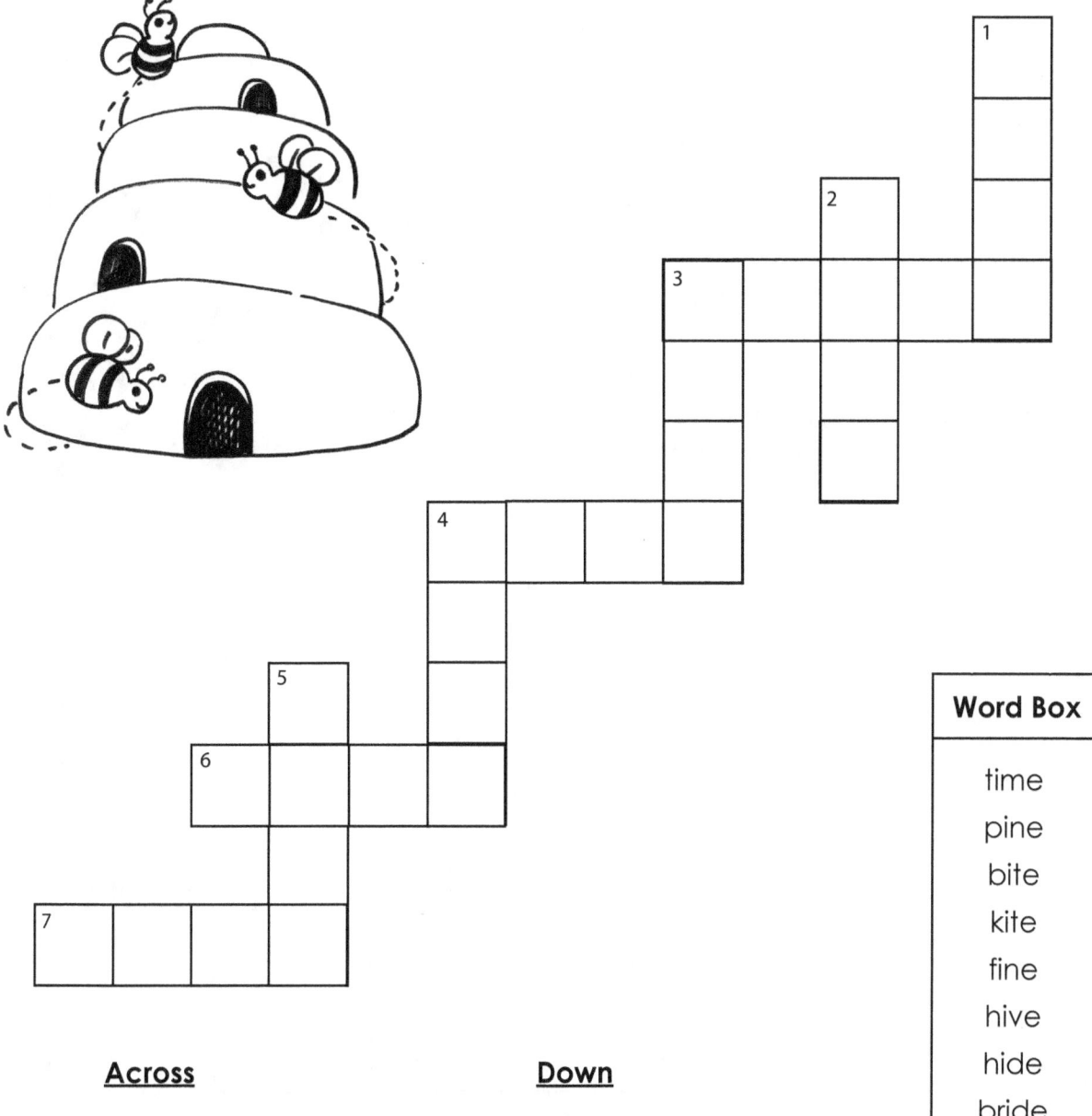

Word Box

time
pine
bite
kite
fine
hive
hide
bride
bike

Across

3. What you call a lady on her wedding day.
4. To go somewhere to avoid having someone find you.
6. Something you fly in the sky using wind.
7. 4 o'clock or 6 o'clock are ways of telling ___.

Down

1. Money you pay for doing something wrong.
2. You use your teeth to ___ something.
3. Something with two wheels that you ride on.
4. A home for bees.
5. A tree that is green in the winter.

Play a game and puzzle answers

Instructions

1. Go to www.starfall.com. Make sure your computer's sound is turned on.
2. Click on "Kindergarten," then on "Learn to Read," and then on the game called "Bike" in Row 8.

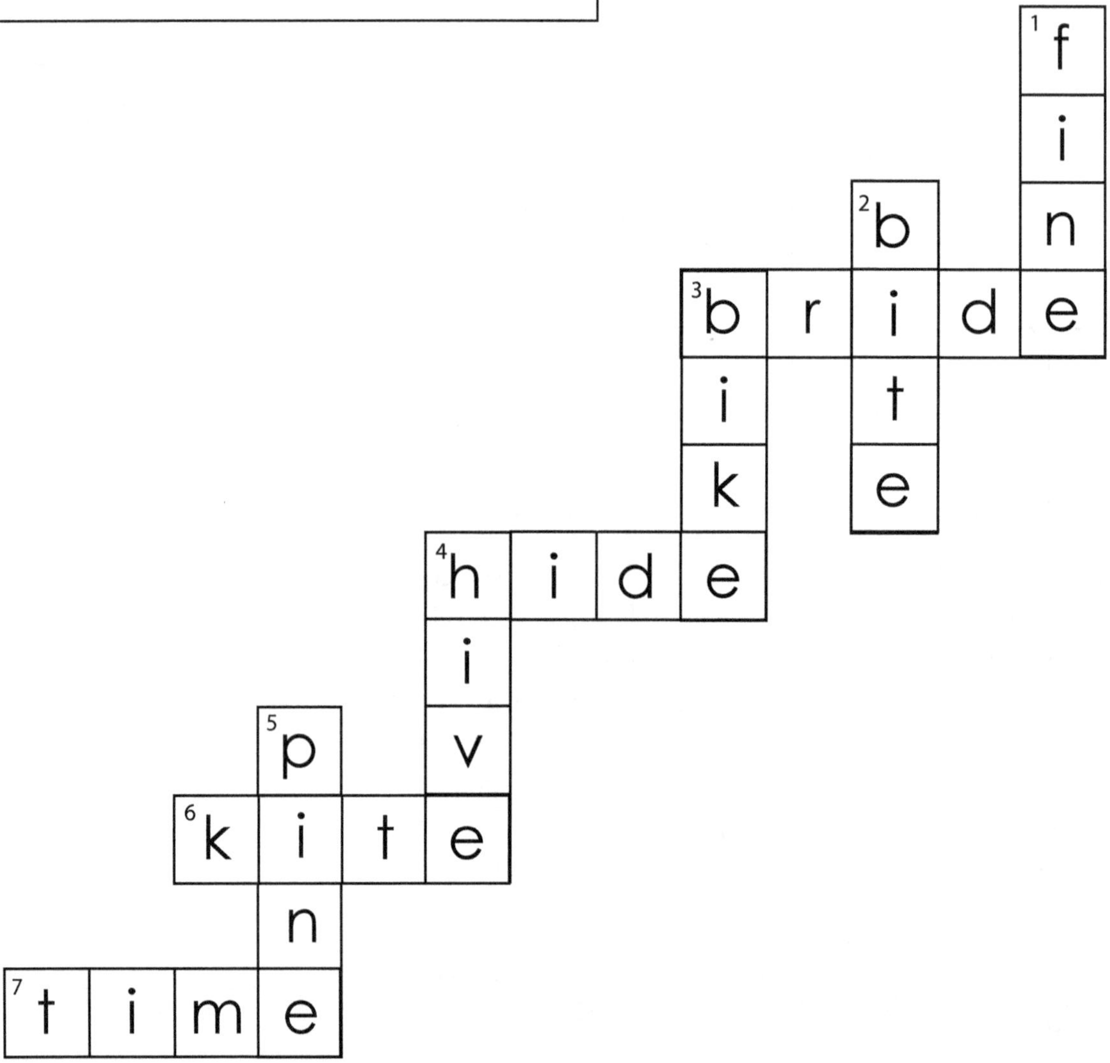

Crossword answers:
1. fine
2. bite
3. bride / bike
4. hide / hive
5. pin
6. kite
7. time

Find the words

The words listed in the box are hidden in the puzzle below. Look for them going down, up, or diagonally. Circle the words when you find them.

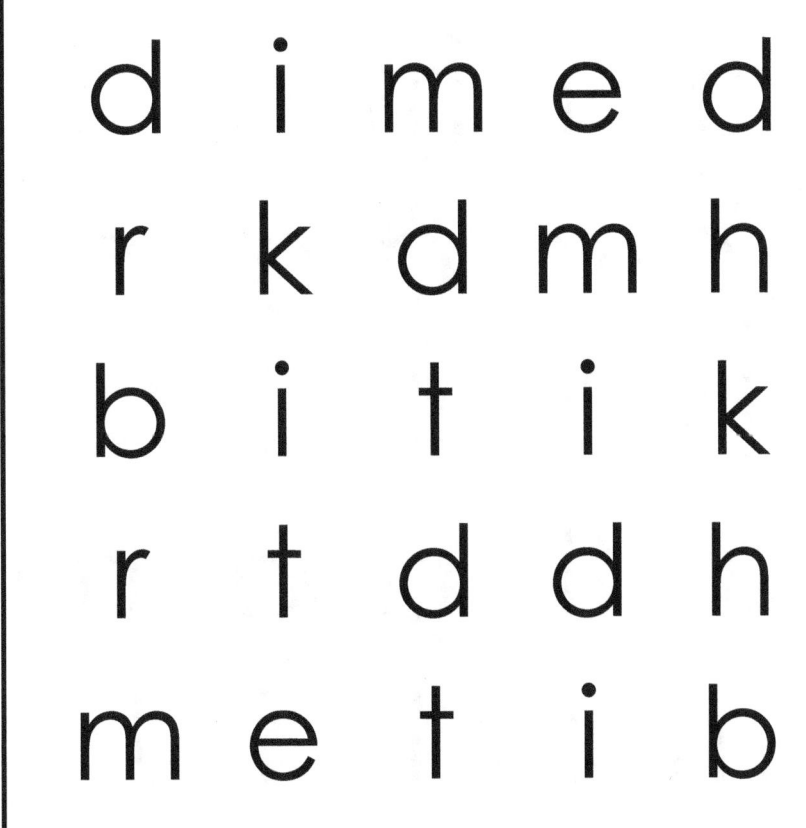

Word box

bit
bite
kit
kite
hid
hide
rid
ride
dim
dime

Answers

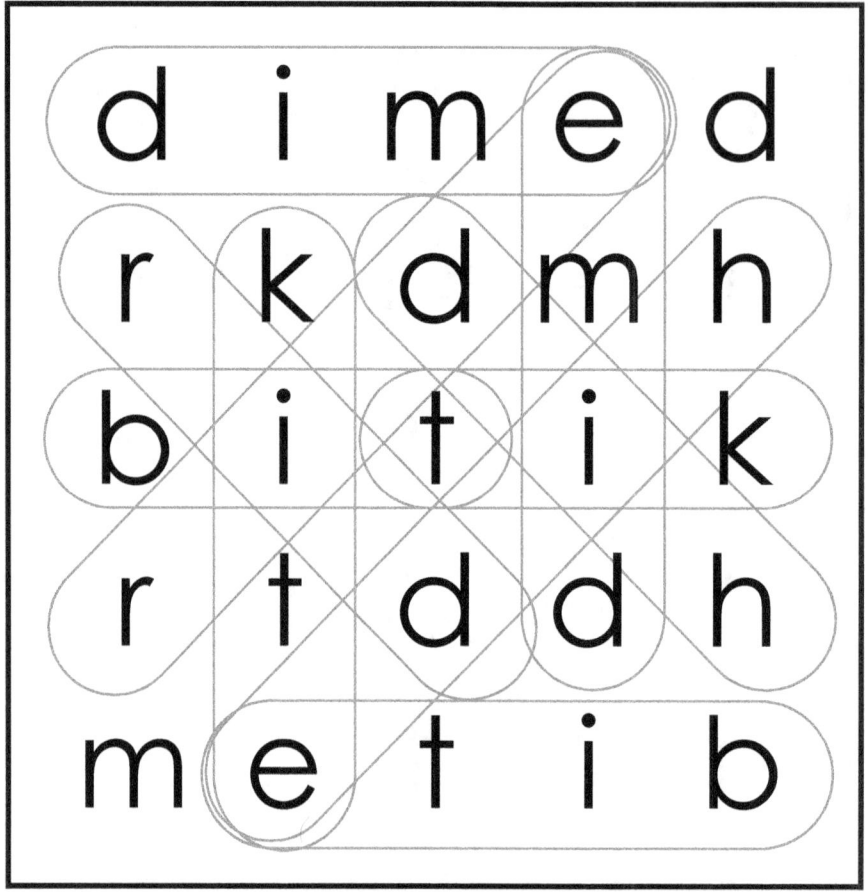

54

Vocabulary

dive

To jump into a pool headfirst.

Example: It is fun to dive into a pool in the summer.

rid

To dispose of.

Example: **He got rid of the garbage.**

dim

Low light.

Example: **The lamp was so dim, that it was hard to see.**

hive

A home for bees.

Example: **The bees made a hive in the tree.**

vine

A plant that attaches itself to trees or fences.
Example: **The vine is pretty.**

55

Read some stories!

Instructions

Read a book

- "Babe, the Bit Hit," by Barbara W. Makar. This is Book 1 in Primary Phonics, Set 2A. See page 1 ("Supplemental Materials") for more information.

- "Mice on Ice," by Nora Gaydos. This is Book 8 in "Now I'm Reading! Level 2: Snack Attack."

Read online

1. Go to www.starfall.com.
2. Click on "Kindergarten," and then on "Learn to Read."
3. Click on Story 8, "Sky Ride," in the column that says, "Book." Make sure the computer's sound is on.
4. Tell the child to read the sentence that appears on the screen for each page. Don't let her click on the individual words because, if she does, the computer will read the words for her. You want the child to do all the reading. After she is done reading each sentence, she can click on the picture above it. The picture will then move in a delightful way.

Step 5   Silent e makes "o" say its name

"o" says its name in "home"

Instructions

Say to the child: **"Silent e makes 'o' say its name in words like 'home,' 'rope,' and 'cone.'"**

Write and read the word

Read	Write silent e on the line	Silent e makes o say its name	Read
hop	hop_e_	hope	hope
mop	mop __	mope	mope
not	not __	note	note
glob	glob __	globe	globe

Which word is it?

Say: "**Read each word out loud. Circle the word that goes with the picture.**"

hop   hope

glob   globe

not   note

mop   mope

cop   cope

Write words in which "o" says its name

Say: **"Write 'o' on the blank lines and read the words out loud."**

c_ne	b_ne
n_te	h_pe
r_pe	p_le
r_be	h_le

Draw a line from the word to the picture

Say: **"Read each word out loud. Then draw a line from the correct word to the picture."**

hose nose those 	cone hum home 
doze rope pole 	not note hope 
pill pull pole 	globe rob robe 

Write the word and circle the picture

Say: "Read the word out loud. Then write the word, and circle the picture that shows the word."

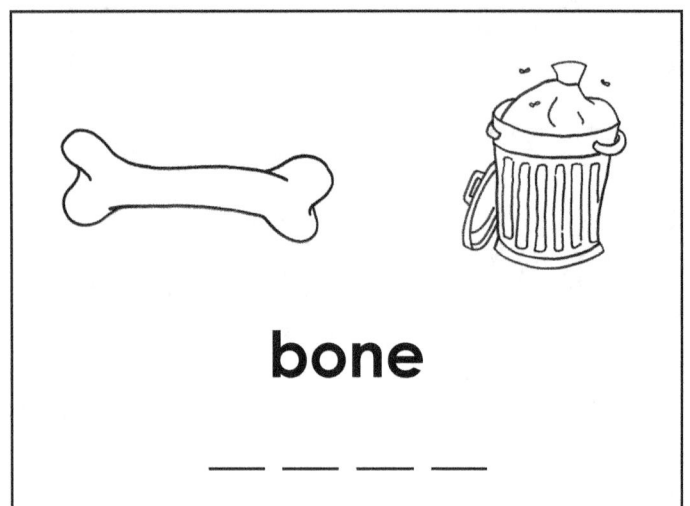

bone

_ _ _ _

doze

_ _ _ _

home

_ _ _ _

cone

_ _ _ _

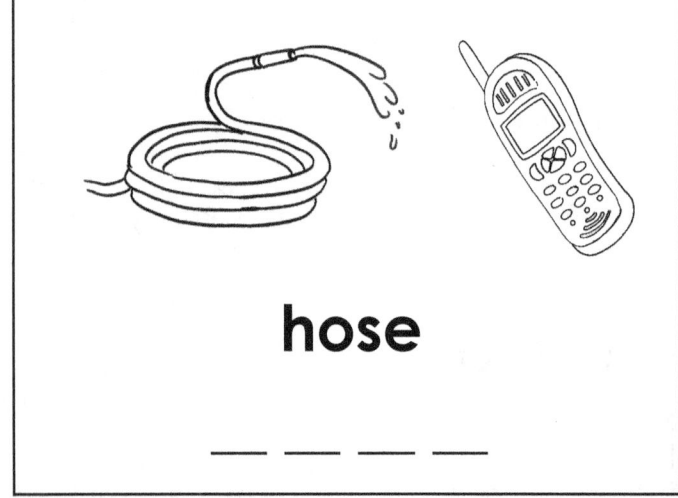

hose

_ _ _ _

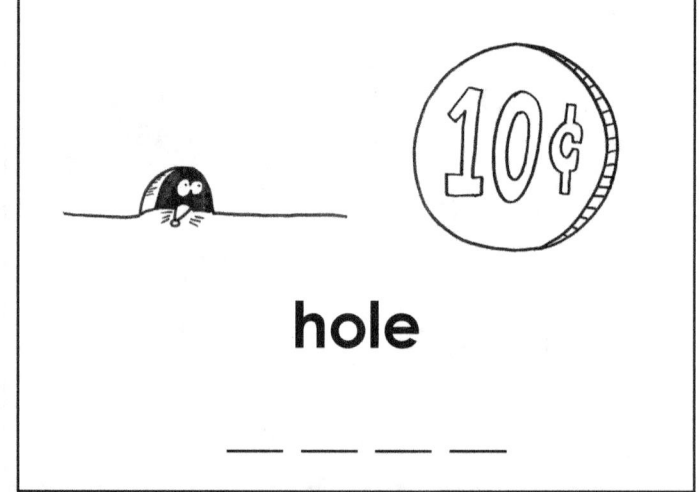

hole

_ _ _ _

Which word is it?

Say: "**Read each word out loud. Circle the word that goes with the picture.**"

rope   hose

hope   home

can   cone

globe   glob

hall   hole

doze   nose

Play Bingo!

Instructions

Materials:
- Flashcards. Cut out the cards on the opposite page.
- 2 gameboards follow the flashcards. In Bingo, every player gets his or her own gameboard. You and the child should each select a gameboard to use.
- Pennies to use as game pieces.

1. Place the flashcards in one stack, with the words facing up.
2. Have the child read the word on the top card in the stack.
3. Each of you should look for that word on your Bingo boards and place a penny on top of the word on your boards when you find it.
4. Place the card the child read face down on the table.
5. Repeat steps 2-4. The child should be the one doing all of the reading of the words on the flashcards. Continue until one of you has five pennies in a row, either horizontally, vertically, or diagonally. The first player to get five in a row should call out, "Bingo!" That player wins the game.

Play Bingo!

bone	hope	vote	note

robe	cone	globe	rope	stone
cope	mope	slope	hope	nose
home	scone	vote	rose	froze
pole	joke	doze	poke	rode

This page is intentionally blank.

This page is intentionally blank.

BINGO

bone	hope	vote	note	robe
cone	globe	rope	stone	cope
mope	slope	✕	hope	nose
home	scone	vote	rose	froze
pole	joke	doze	poke	rode

BINGO

robe	slope	mope	vote	globe
home	bone	stone	scone	cope
note	vote	✕	cone	pole
doze	poke	hope	rope	nose
rode	hope	froze	joke	rose

Step 6   Power Word

want

want

want

want

Does the sentence make sense?

Say: "**Read each sentence out loud. Color in the smiley face if the sentence makes sense, and the frown if it does not.**"

I want to bike with a pal.	☺	☹

Do you want some cake on your cone?	☺	☹

I want a hive on my dish.	☺	☹

Do you want a cake in your cup?	☺	☹

I want to bite the kite.	☺	☹

Do you want to come to the lake?	☺	☹

I want a chip for a snack.	☺	☹

Do you want to swim with a shell?	☺	☹

Play a board game!

First one to reach the end wins!

Instructions

<u>Materials you will need</u>:
- A single die.
- Coins to use as markers.
- Gameboard, *opposite page*.

1. Each player places a coin on "start."
2. Take turns rolling the die.
3. Move forward the same amount of spaces as the number on the die.
4. As you move forward on the board, read the words that you pass and land on.
5. For example, if a five comes up on the die, move five spaces on the game board and read five words.
6. The first person to reach the end wins.

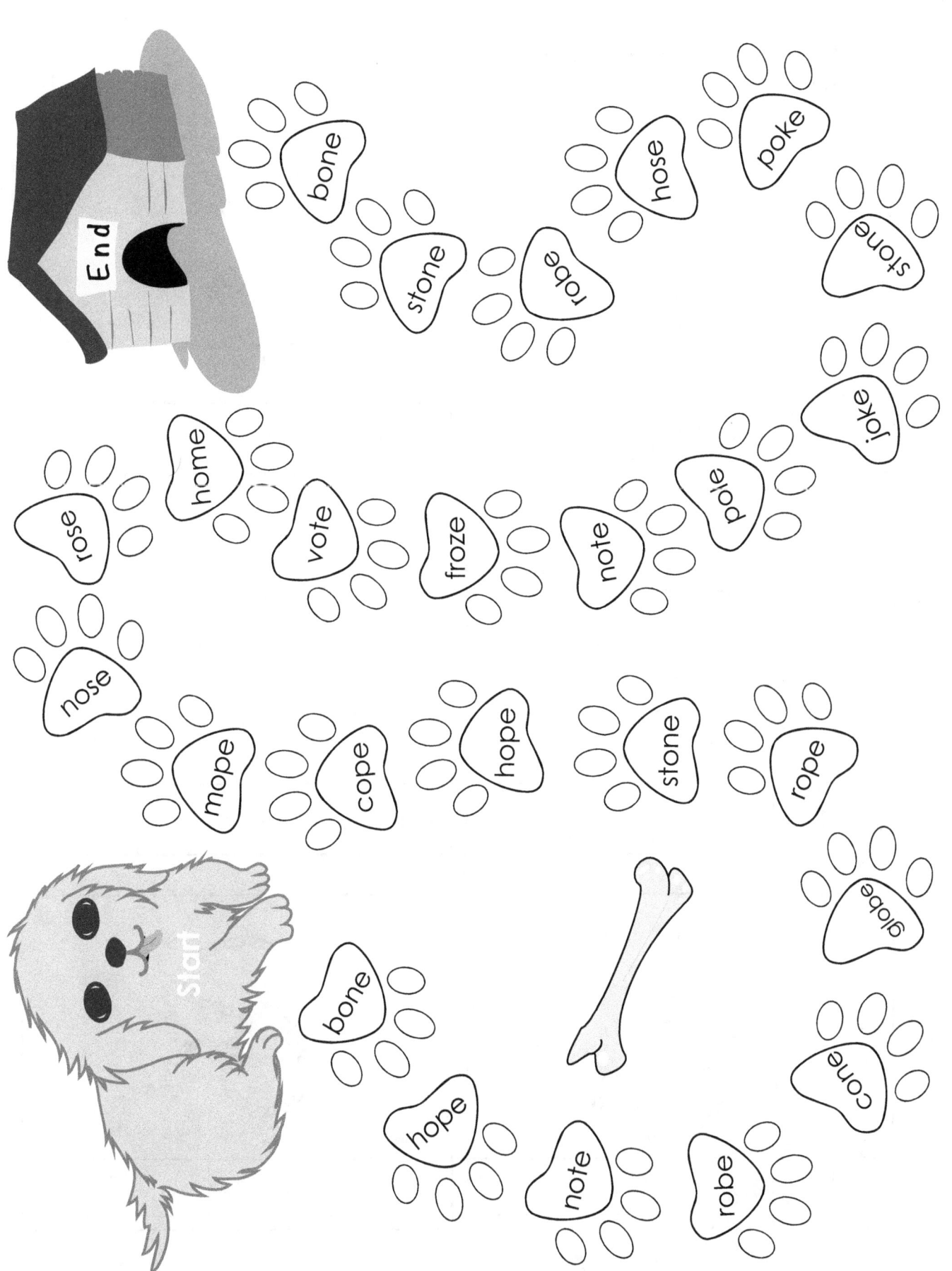

Circle the letters

Say: "**Circle the correct letters. Then write the word.**"
Tell the child the pictures show: robe, rose, cone, doze, home, rope.

(r) m r (o) x (b) m (e)   r o b e

f r o i v s h e   _ _ _ _

c s o i x n m e   _ _ _ _

d c i o t z m e   _ _ _ _

h s h o v m e p   _ _ _ _

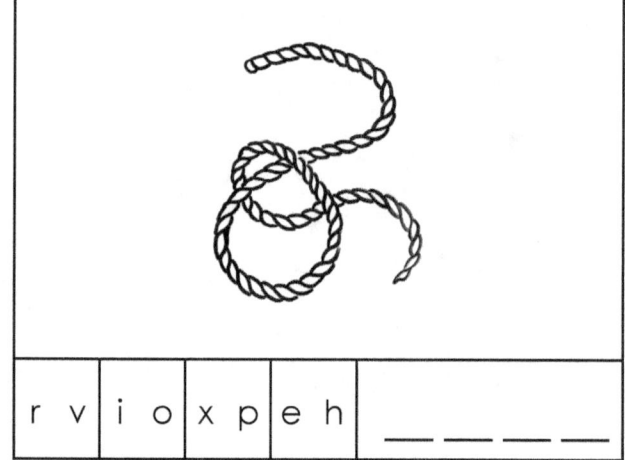

r v i o x p e h   _ _ _ _

74

Solve the puzzle

Word Box

robe
hope
note
rose
home
bone
hole
cone
doze

Across

3. Something a dog likes to chew.
4. Something you dig.
6. To wish something will happen.
7. Something you put on after a shower.

Down

1. To sleep lightly.
2. Ice cream is served on top of this.
4. The place you live.
5. Something you write down.
7. A type of flower.

Play a game and puzzle answers

> **Instructions**
>
> 1. Go to www.starfall.com.
> Make sure your computer's sound is turned on.
> 2. Click on "Kindergarten," then "Learn to Read."
> 3. Go to Row 9 and click on the game labeled "Long o."
> 4. Have your student play this coloring activity.
> 5. Then go back to Row 9 and click on the game called "Nose."

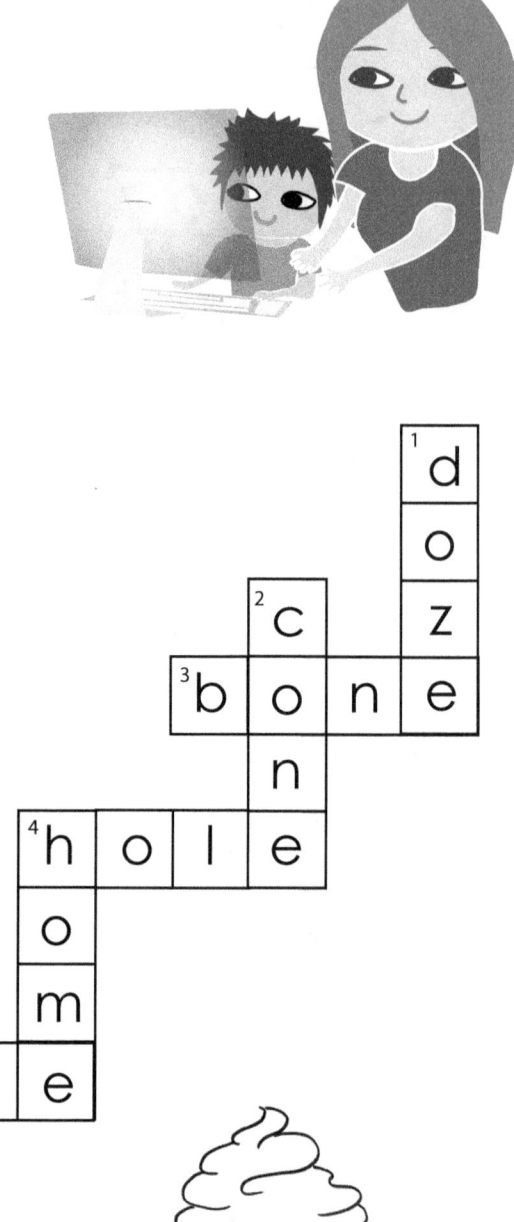

Find the words

The words listed in the box are hidden in the puzzle below. Look for them going down, up, or diagonally. Circle the words when you find them.

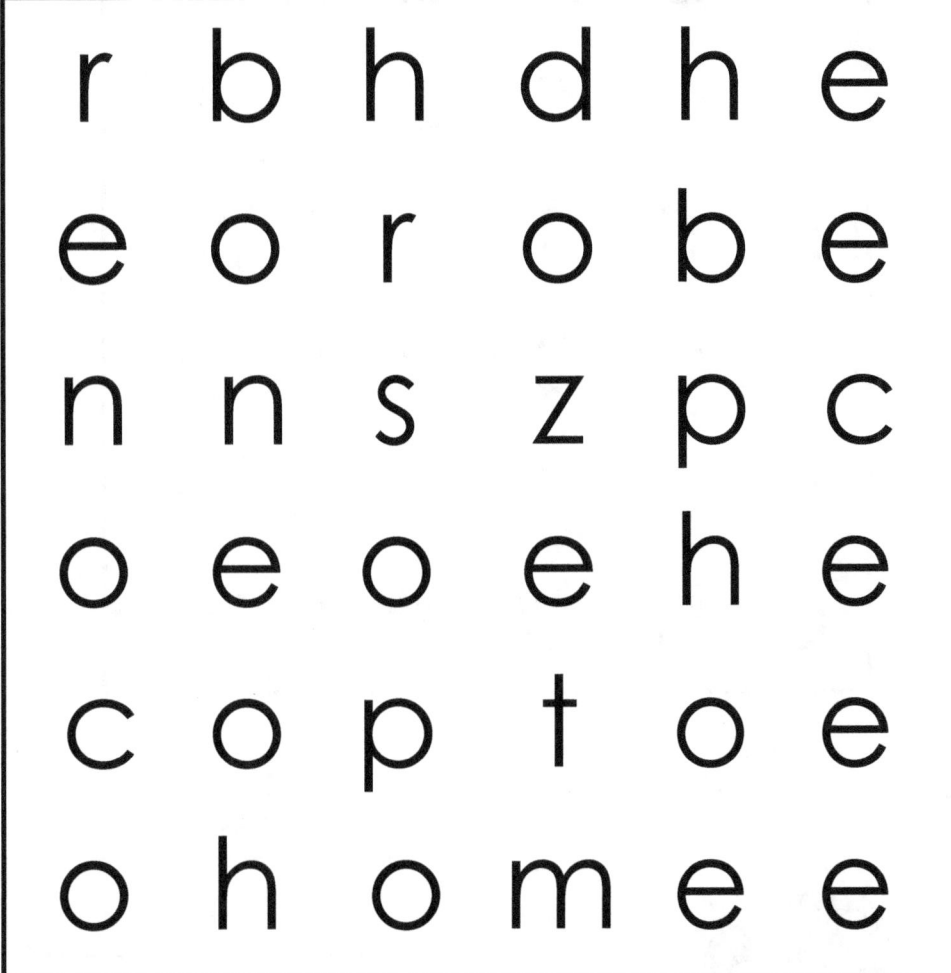

Word box
home
note
bone
rose
doze
hope
robe
cone

Read some stories and puzzle answers

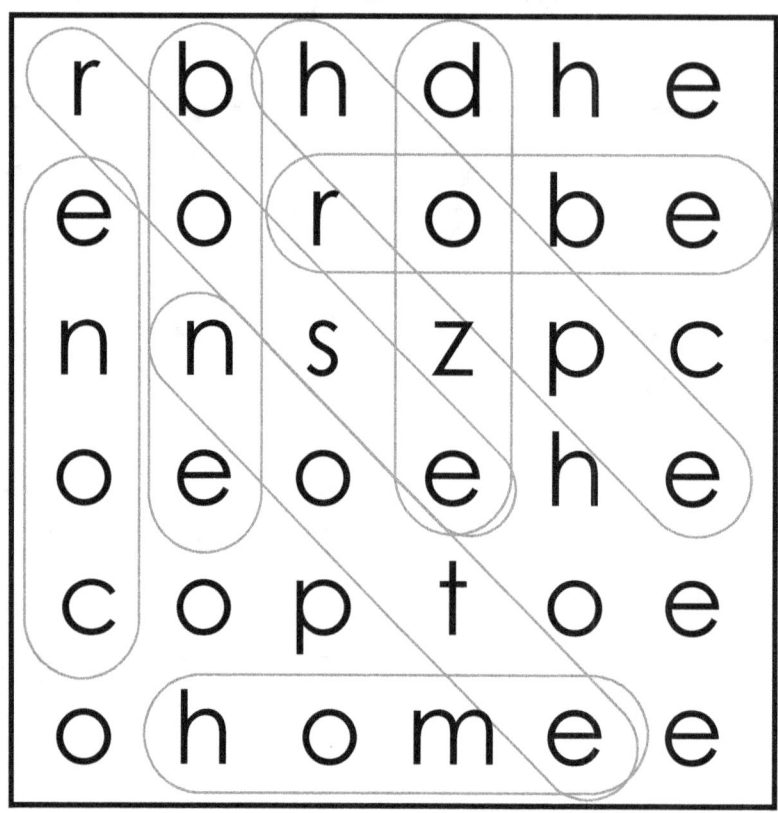

Instructions

Read a book

The child can now read:

- "A Ride on a Bus," by Barbara W. Makar. This is Book A in Primary Phnoics, Set 2A.
- "Mole," by Barbara W. Makar. This is Book 3 in Primary Phonics, Set 2A. See pg. 1 ("Supplementary Materials") for more information.

Step 7 Silent e makes "u" say its name

'u' says its name in "cute"

Instructions

Say to the child: **"Silent e makes 'u' say its name in words like 'cute,' 'cube,' and 'huge.'"**

Write and read the word

Read	Write silent e on the line	Silent e makes u say its name	Read
us	us e	use	use
cut	cut __	cute	cute
hug	hug __	huge	huge
cub	cub __	cube	cube
mull	mul __	mule	mule
puck	puk __	puke	puke
tub	tub __	tube	tube

Which word is it?

Say: "**Read each word out loud. Circle the word that goes with the picture.**"

hug   huge

cut   cute

use   us

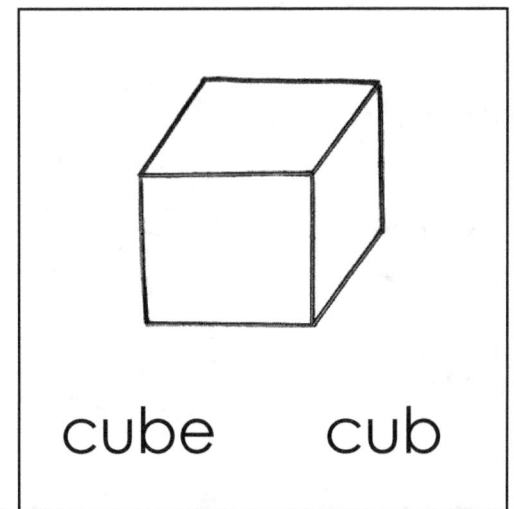

cube   cub

mule   mull

tub   tube

Draw a line from the word to the picture

Say: "**Read each word out loud. Then draw a line from the correct word to the picture.**"

cute
cut
cube
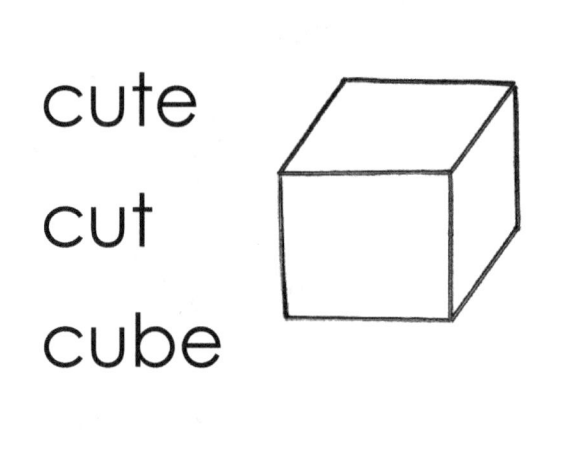

cube
puke
cute

mule
huge
hug

use
bus
us

tube
tub
mule

full
mule
huge

Solve the puzzle!

Word Box

huge
mule
use
us
cute
cube
cub
cut
mull
hug

Across

1. What you do with scissors.
2. Square in shape.
5. Very big.
6. To put your arms around someone you like.
7. The opposite of just letting something sit on a shelf.

Down

1. A baby bear.
2. Adorable.
3. An animal that can pull heavy loads.
4. To think something over.
7. You and me.

Puzzle answers

84

Write the word and circle the picture

Say: "Read the word out loud. Then write it and circle the picture that shows the word."

tube

— — — —

cute

— — — —

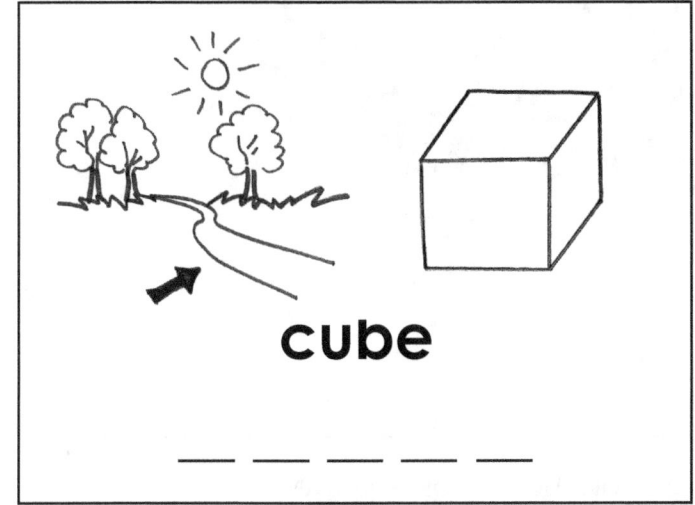

cube

— — — —

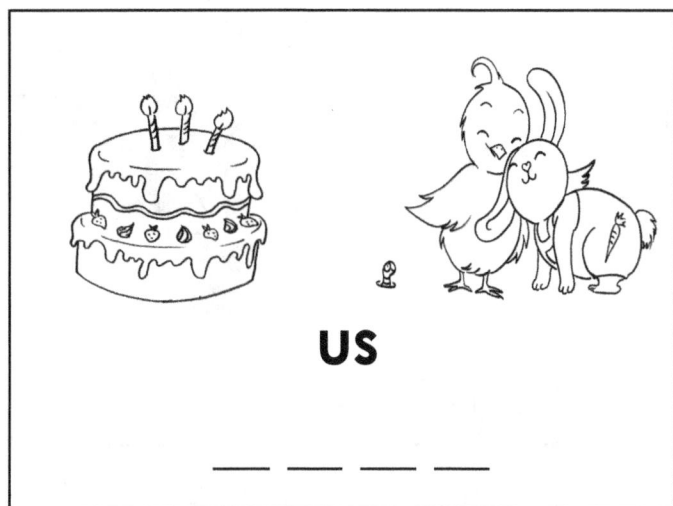

us

— —

mule

— — — —

huge

— — — —

85

Play Bingo!

Instructions

Materials: • Flashcards. Cut out the cards on the opposite page.
• 2 gameboards follow the flashcards. In Bingo, every player gets his or her own gameboard. You and the child should each select a gameboard to use.
• Pennies to use as game pieces.

1. Place the flashcards in one stack, with the words facing up.
2. Have the child read the word on the top card in the stack.
3. Each of you should look for that word on your Bingo boards and place a penny on top of the word on your boards when you find it.
4. Place the card the child read face down on the table.
5. Repeat steps 2-4. The child should be the one doing all of the reading of the words on the flashcards. Continue until one of you has five pennies in a row, either horizontally, vertically, or diagonally. The first player to get five in a row should call out, "Bingo!" That player wins the game.

Play Bingo!

use	cane	fine	mule	
hope	note	cube	nose	Pete
tube	cake	hike	stone	game
kite	cute	home	huge	joke
line	poke	shave	time	ripe

This page is intentionally blank.

This page is intentionally blank.

BINGO

cane	kite	mule	Pete	nose
cute	fine	home	tube	huge
note	cake	✕	line	hope
joke	stone	use	poke	game
cube	shave	ripe	hike	time

BINGO

kite	hope	line	mule	poke
cane	joke	stone	game	use
cute	fine	✗	note	hike
cube	shave	nose	Pete	time
home	tube	cake	huge	ripe

Step 8 — Power Word

some
come
some
come

Write the Word

some

come

some

come

some

come

Does the sentence make sense?

Say: "**Read each sentence out loud. Color in the smiley face if the sentence makes sense, and the frown if it does not.**"

Come to the lake and have some fun! ☺ ☹

Did the dog put some socks in the wash? ☺ ☹

Can a cute dog come home? ☺ ☹

The tube did pinch some cans. ☺ ☹

Did the fish come to save the man? ☺ ☹

The cat ate some chips and dip. ☺ ☹

Will the duck have some chips in a cup? ☺ ☹

Can a lake ask some fish to come home? ☺ ☹

Find the words

The words listed in the box are hidden in the puzzle below. Look for them going down, up, or diagonally. Circle the words when you find them.

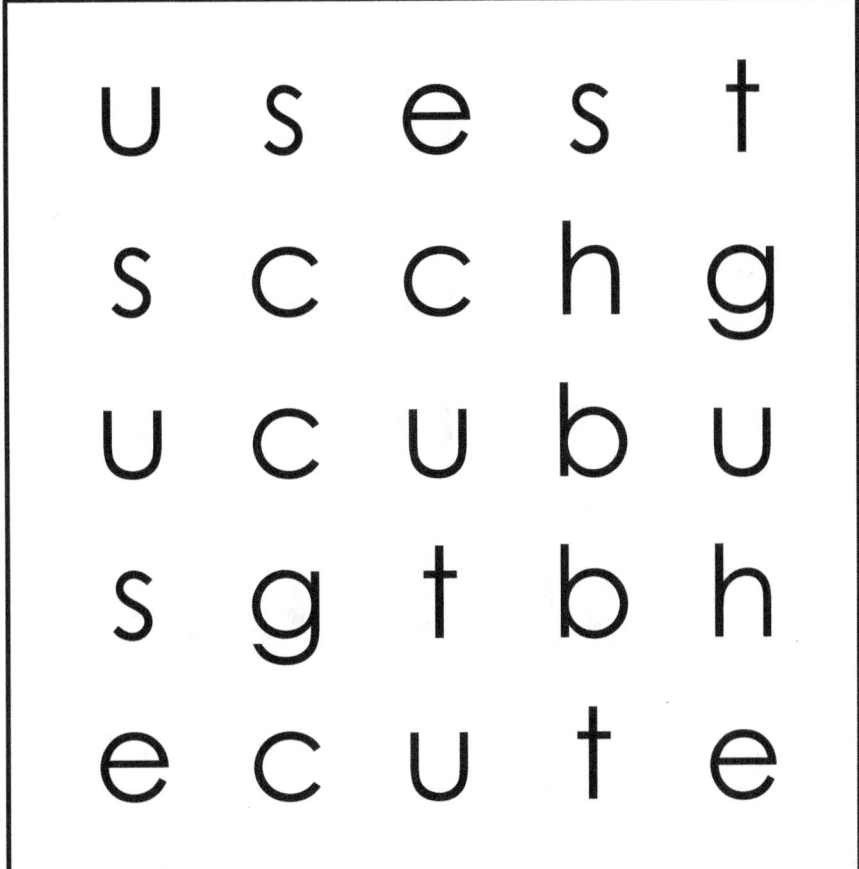

Word box

cut
cute
cub
cube
hug
huge
us
use

Puzzle answers

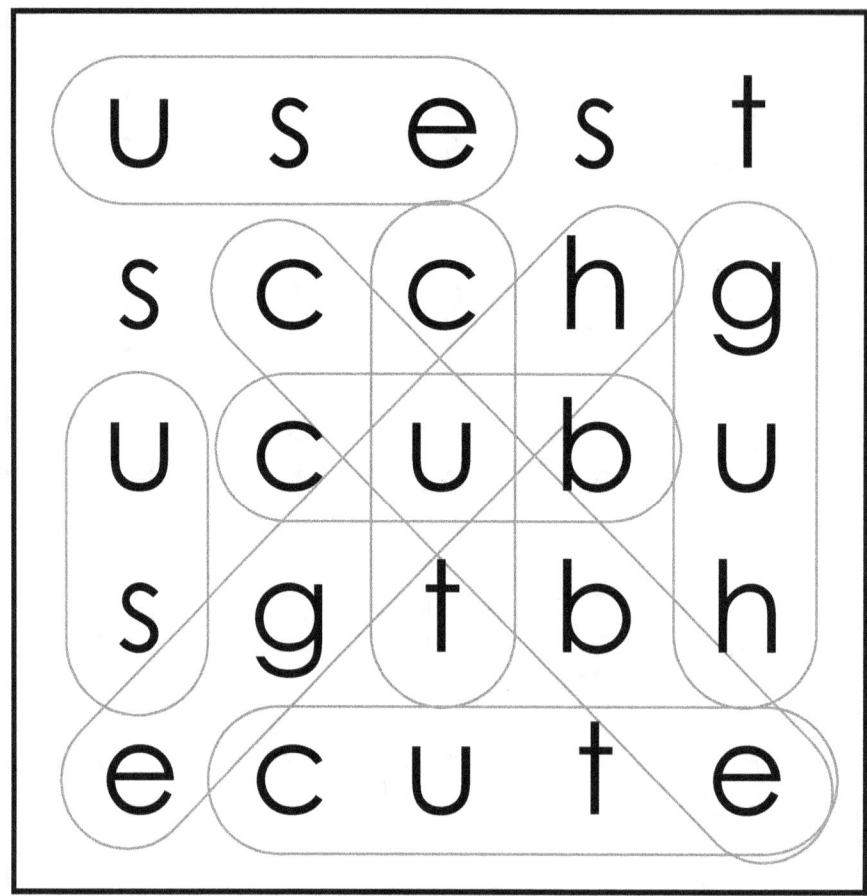

Vocabulary

globe
A ball-shaped map of the world.

doze

To sleep lighlty.

mope
To sulk or be sad.

mull
To think for a long time.

mule

A cross between a donkey and a horse.

robe

Something you wear after a bath.

Play a board game!

Instructions

Materials you will need:
- A single die.
- Coins to use as markers.
- Gameboard, *opposite page*.

1. Each player places a coin on "start."
2. Take turns rolling the die.
3. Move forward the same amount of spaces as the number on the die.
4. As you move forward on the board, read the words that you pass and land on.
5. For example, if a five comes up on the die, move five spaces on the game board and read five words.
6. The first person to reach the end wins.

Step 9   Vowels at the end of little words

Instructions

Say: "**Vowels say their names at the end of little words like** "hi," "no," and "we.'"

Circle the vowels

Say: **"Read each word out loud and circle the vowel in each word."**

Which word is it?

Say: **"Read each word out loud. Circle the word that goes with the picture."**

me   we

he   hi

he   hi

we   me

go   so

be   no

Write the word and circle the picture

Say: "**Read the word out loud. Then write it, and circle the picture that shows the word.**"

no

___ ___

go

___ ___

he

___ ___

we

___ ___

hi

___ ___

yo-yo

___ ___ ___ ___

Play games on the computer!

Instructions

1. Go to www.starfall.com. Make sure your computer's sound is turned on.
2. Click on "Kindergarten" and then "Learn to Read."
3. In "Learn to Read, the right-hand column is labeled, "Movies." Go to row #10 and click on the "Video" link labeled "Lonely Vowel."
4. Watch this short skit about vowels at the end of little words.

Draw a line from the word to the picture

Say: "**Read each word out loud. Then draw a line from the correct word to the picture.**"

he me see	be go we
he hi yo-yo	he see be
go yo-yo no	so no go

Play a board game!

First one to reach the end wins!

Instructions

Materials you will need:
- A single die.
- Coins to use as markers.
- Gameboard, *opposite page*.

1. Each player places a coin on "start."
2. Take turns rolling the die.
3. Move forward the same amount of spaces as the number on the die.
4. As you move forward on the board, read the words that you pass and land on.
5. For example, if a five comes up on the die, move five spaces on the game board and read five words.
6. The first person to reach the end wins.

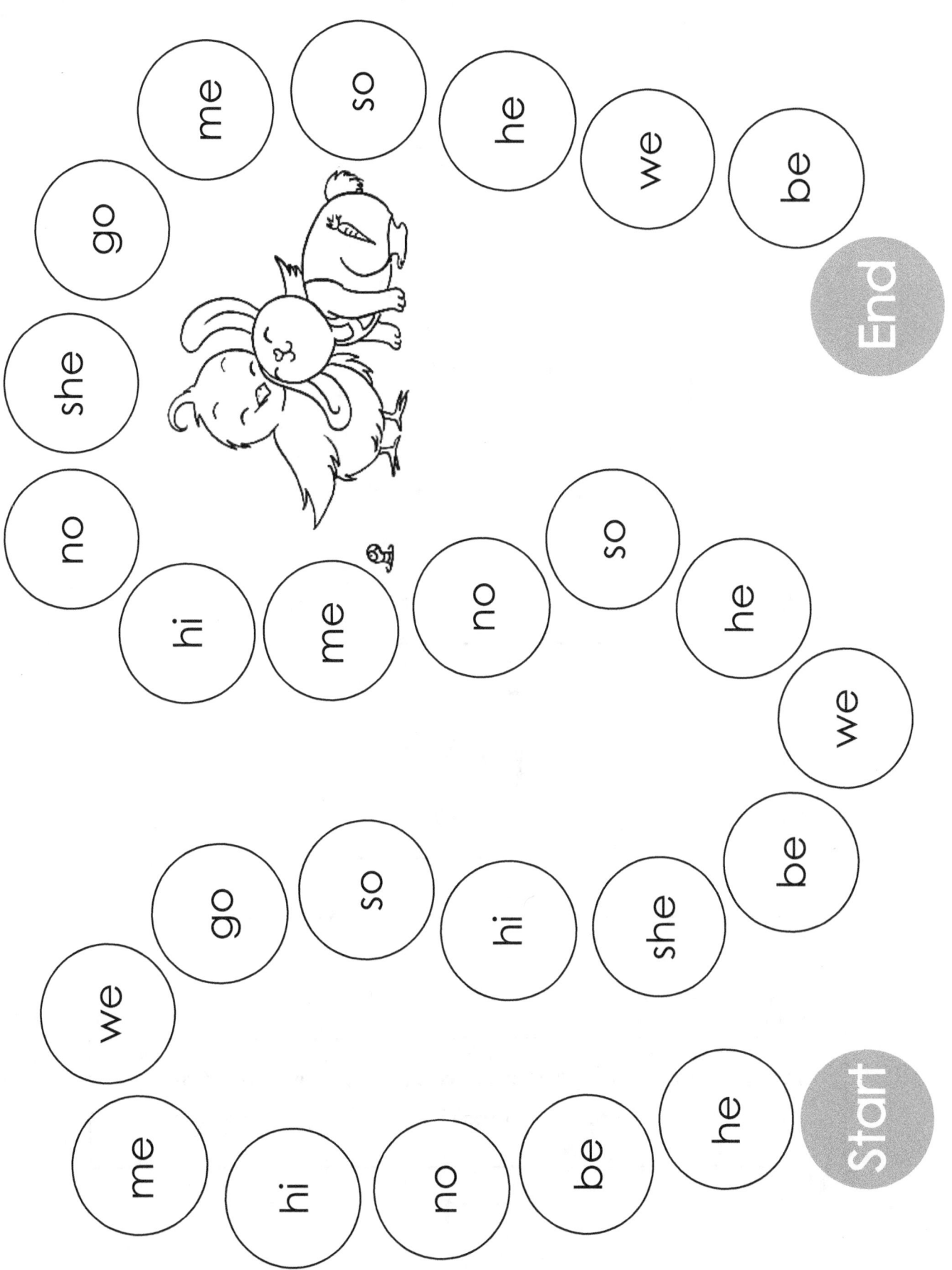

Step 10　　　　　　　　y at the end of a word

Instructions

Say to the child: **"Y at the end of a little word says the letter i's name in words like 'my,' 'why,' and 'dry.'"**

Which word is it?

Say: "**Read each word out loud. Circle the word that goes with the picture.**"

cry   try

why   fly

by   sky

fry   try

spy   cry

shy   dry

Write the word and circle the picture

Say: **"Read the word out loud. Then write the word, and circle the picture that shows the word."**

spy

___ ___ ___

sky

___ ___ ___

fly

___ ___ ___

dry

___ ___ ___

cry

___ ___ ___

fry

___ ___ ___

Draw a line from the word to the picture

Say: "**Read each word out loud. Then draw a line from the correct word to the picture.**"

fly fry try 	try dry why 
my cry by 	shy why sky 
by my spy 	fly fry shy 

Play Bingo!

Instructions

Materials:
- Flashcards. Cut out the cards on the opposite page.
- 2 gameboards follow the flashcards. In Bingo, every player gets his or her own gameboard. You and the child should each select a gameboard to use.
- Pennies to use as game pieces.

1. Place the flashcards in one stack, with the words facing up.
2. Have the child read the word on the top card in the stack.
3. Each of you should look for that word on your Bingo boards and place a penny on top of the word on your boards when you find it.
4. Place the card the child read face down on the table.
5. Repeat steps 2-4. The child should be the one doing all of the reading of the words on the flashcards. Continue until one of you has three pennies in a row, either horizontally, vertically, or diagonally. The first player to get three in a row should call out, "Bingo!" That player wins the game.

Bingo Flashcards

Cut out the cards along the dotted lines.

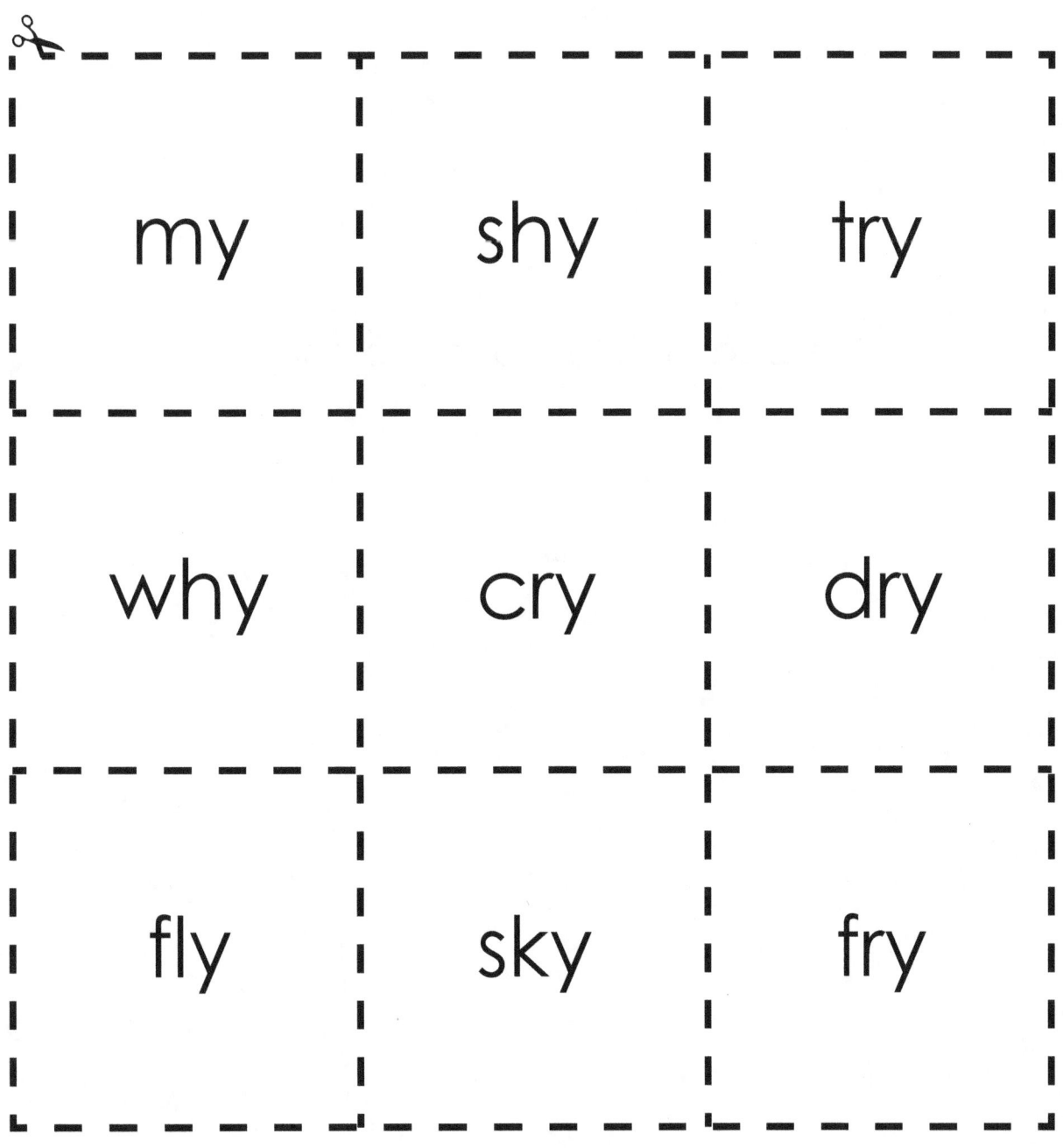

113

This page is intentionally blank.

This page is intentionally blank.

BINGO

shy	dry	why
cry	sky	my
try	fry	fly

BINGO

my	shy	try
why	cry	dry
fly	sky	fry

Step 11   y at the end of a longer word

bunny

Instructions

Say to the child: **"Y at the end of a longer word says e's name as in the words `bunny', `puppy,' and `lucky.'"**

Which word is it?

Say: "**Read each word out loud. Circle the word that goes with the picture.**"

mommy   funny

sloppy   candy

bunny   lucky

happy   fancy

very   puppy

penny   berry

Circle the letters

Say: **"Circle the correct letters. Then write the word."**
Tell the child the pictures show: baby, Mommy, and bunny.

| b | m | r | a | x | b | m | y | b a b y |

| M | S | c | o | o | m | m | n | m | y | _ _ _ _ _ |

| b | s | u | o | o | n | m | n | m | y | _ _ _ _ _ |

120

Circle the letters

Say: **"Circle the correct letters. Then write the word."**
Tell the child the pictures show: happy, puppy, and Daddy.

| h | s | c | a | o | p | m | p | m | y | _ _ _ _ _ |

| p | s | u | o | o | p | p | n | m | y | _ _ _ _ _ |

| D | S | u | a | o | d | m | d | m | y | _ _ _ _ _ |

Draw a line from the word to the picture

Say: "**Read each word out loud. Then draw a line from the correct word to the picture.**"

Nancy
baby
fancy

happy
sloppy
Henry

jumpy
grumpy
bunny

very
candy
Mommy

penny
chilly
silly

cherry
copy
puppy

Write the word and circle the picture

Say: "Read the word out loud. Then write it, and circle the picture that shows the word."

penny

_ _ _ _ _

bunny

_ _ _ _ _

happy

_ _ _ _ _

baby

_ _ _ _

puppy

_ _ _ _ _

candy

_ _ _ _ _

Play Bingo!

Instructions

Materials:
- Flashcards. Cut out the cards on the opposite page.
- 2 gameboards follow the flashcards. In Bingo, every player gets his or her own gameboard. You and the child should each select a gameboard to use.
- Pennies to use as game pieces.

1. Place the flashcards in one stack, with the words facing up.
2. Have the child read the word on the top card in the stack.
3. Each of you should look for that word on your Bingo boards and place a penny on top of the word on your boards when you find it.
4. Place the card the child read face down on the table.
5. Repeat steps 2-4. The child should be the one doing all of the reading of the words on the flashcards. Continue until one of you has five pennies in a row, either horizontally, vertically, or diagonally. The first player to get five in a row should call out, "Bingo!" That player wins the game.

Play Bingo!

baby	funny	puppy	pony

bunny	penny	berry	lucky	happy
Mommy	candy	sunny	very	chilly
Billy	grumpy	jumpy	Daddy	fancy
silly	cherry	belly	body	windy

This page is intentionally blank.

This page is intentionally blank.

BINGO

baby	funny	puppy	pony	bunny
penny	berry	lucky	happy	Mommy
candy	sunny	✗	very	chilly
Billy	grumpy	jumpy	Daddy	fancy
silly	cherry	belly	body	windy

BINGO

bunny	Billy	jumpy	lucky	candy
very	silly	baby	Mommy	fancy
funny	grumpy	✗	cherry	pony
Daddy	berry	puppy	penny	body
happy	windy	belly	sunny	chilly

Step 12   Power Word

could

would

could

would

Does the sentence make sense?

Say: "**Read each sentence out loud. Color in the smiley face if the sentence makes sense, and the frown if it does not.**"

	☺ ☹
Could a baby make a funny face?	☺ ☹
Would a puppy try to bake a cake?	☺ ☹
Could a lucky penny bring some luck?	☺ ☹
Would a cute bunny be happy with candy?	☺ ☹
Could a fly cry, "Why not try?"	☺ ☹
Would a baby hug his mommy?	☺ ☹
Could the shy fly dry the sky?	☺ ☹
Would a daddy try to spy on a fly?	☺ ☹

Play a board game!

Instructions

<u>Materials you will need</u>:
- A single die.
- Coins to use as markers.
- Gameboard, *opposite page*.

1. Each player places a coin on "start."
2. Take turns rolling the die.
3. Move forward the same amount of spaces as the number on the die.
4. As you move forward on the board, read the words that you pass and land on.
5. For example, if a five comes up on the die, move five spaces on the game board and read five words and/or sounds.
6. The first person to reach the end wins.

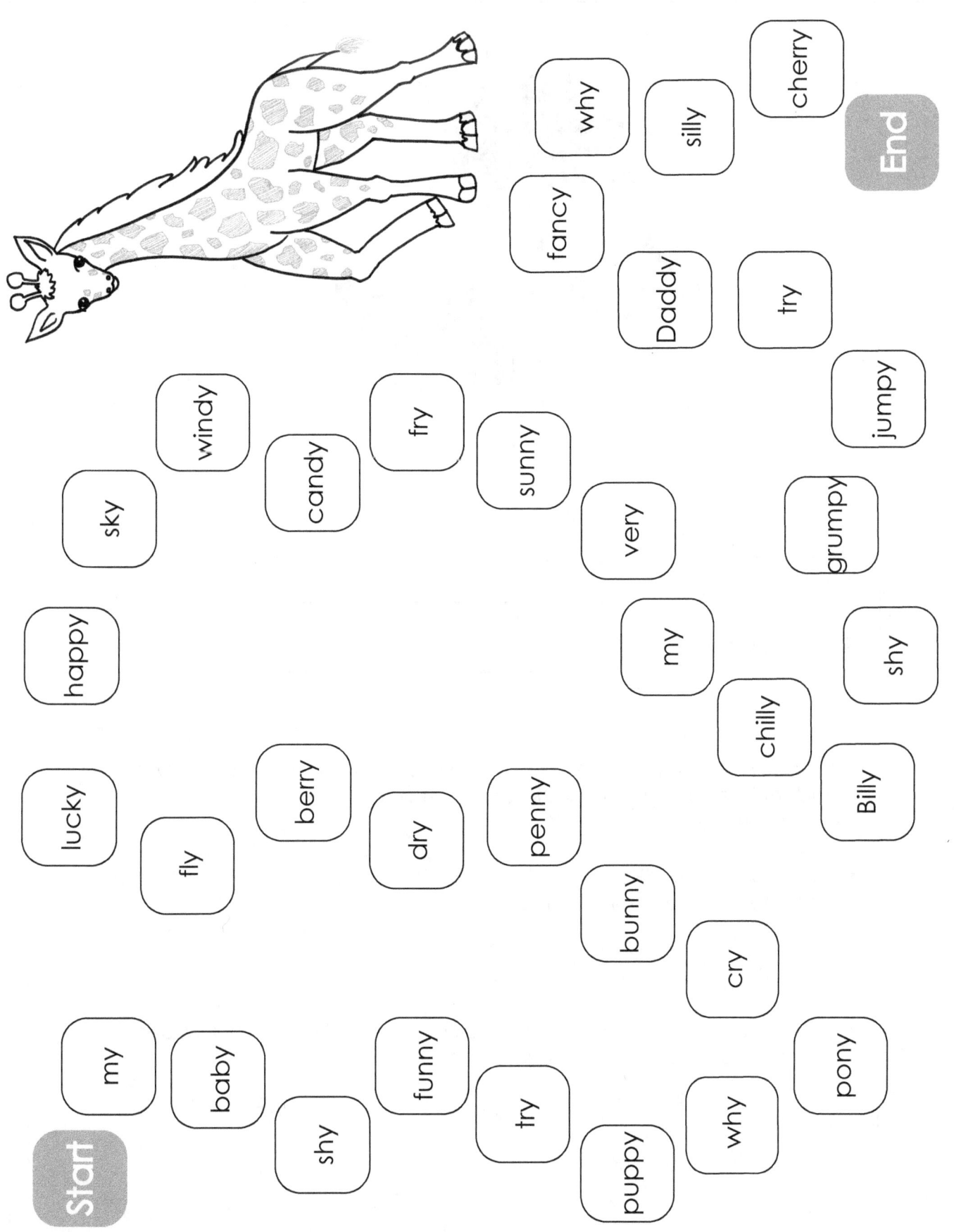

Read some stories!

Instructions

Read a book

- "Dishy-Washy," by Joy Crowley. There are a few words in the story your student has not yet learned. Read those words to your student when he or she reaches them.

- "Go, Go, Go." (A "Read with Dick and Jane" book.) Have your student read the first three stories in this little book. They are:
    - "Go, Go, Go"
    - "Sally and Mother"
    - "The Boat Go Howl"

- "Go Away, Spot." (A "Read with Dick and Jane" book.) Your student will be able to read all four stories in this book.

Power word review

	some
do	come
you	could
want	would

135

This page is intentionally blank.

Congratulations!
You've completed Step 4 in reading!

Certificate of Accomplishment

Presented to _____

Signed: _____

Date: _____